CATALOGING CORRECTLY
FOR KIDS

SIXTH EDITION

CATALOGING
CORRECTLY
FOR KIDS

An Introduction to the Tools and Practices

EDITED BY
Michele Zwierski, Joanna F. Fountain,
AND **Marilyn McCroskey**

ALA
Editions
CHICAGO | 2021

ISBNs
978-0-8389-1871-5 (paper)
978-0-8389-4994-8 (PDF)
978-0-8389-4995-5 (ePub)

Library of Congress Cataloging-in-Publication Data
Names: Zwierski, Michele, editor. | Fountain, Joanna F., editor. | McCroskey, Marilyn, editor.
Title: Cataloging correctly for kids : an introduction to the tools and practices / edited by Michele Zwierski, Joanna F. Fountain, Marilyn McCroskey.
Description: Sixth edition. | Chicago : ALA Editions, 2021. | Includes bibliographical references and index. | Summary: "The sixth edition guides catalogers, children's librarians, and LIS students in taking an effective approach towards materials intended for children and young adults. Informed by recent studies of how children search, this handbook's top-to-bottom revisions address areas such as how RDA applies to a variety of children's materials, with examples provided; authority control, bibliographic description, subject access, and linked data; electronic resources and other non-book materials; and cataloging for non-English-speaking and preliterate children"—Provided by publisher.
Identifiers: LCCN 2020047120 (print) | LCCN 2020047121 (ebook) | ISBN 9780838918715 (paperback) | ISBN 9780838949948 (pdf) | ISBN 9780838949955 (epub)
Subjects: LCSH: Cataloging of children's literature. | Cataloging of children's literature—United States.
Classification: LCC Z695.1.C6 C37 2021 (print) | LCC Z695.1.C6 (ebook) | DDC 025.3/2—dc23
LC record available at https://lccn.loc.gov/2020047120
LC ebook record available at https://lccn.loc.gov/2020047121

Book design by Alejandra Diaz in the Odile, Proxima and Museo Slab and Roboto typefaces.

♾ This paper meets the requirements of ANSI/NISO Z39.48-1992 (Permanence of Paper).

Printed in the United States of America
25 24 23 22 21   5 4 3 2 1

CONTENTS

INTRODUCTION

Welcome to the sixth edition of *Cataloging Correctly for Kids: An Introduction to the Tools and Practices*. When this handbook was originally published in 1989, the majority of library services were firmly centered around collections that were mostly print. Library collections for children, however, even before 1989, included materials (especially those in schools) that were filled with cutting-edge nonprint materials. Traditional library collections began to expand and change, adding new formats and embracing new technology. The cataloging world changed too, transforming rules to accommodate this ever-expanding world of library materials. Everything changes, but our mission as cataloging librarians remains the same as it was in 1989: to provide consistent, accurate, rich data for discovery.

Children's library materials are used by children, educators, and parents. What are the needs of these diverse user groups? Children might want to read a good book; educators might need topical resources for specific grade and/or reading levels; parents might be looking for materials to expand learning and enjoyment for their child. All these expectations (and more) can be met with a thoughtfully crafted bibliographic record.

The steps in quality cataloging involve many complex rules and decisions, so we have provided targeted chapters that explain rules and processes and the logic behind them. We hope to present basic cataloging concepts to you in a simple, practical way.

To build a library catalog, use the understanding you already have of the needs of your users. A catalog, under some circumstances, will be the surrogate for you, the live librarian. It is important to consider these basic informational needs when cataloging each item. Reality, however, can thwart good intentions. Inadequate staffing, funding, and scheduling all can push any librarian to allocate little or no time to cataloging.

Each chapter in this book includes time-saving suggestions and low- or no-cost tools. Our authors have created many cataloging records and are experts in creating the best record as efficiently and economically as possible.

As a provider of library services to children, you already know how your community asks for materials. All your experience can be translated and crafted into rich bibliographic records. Cataloging is but one of the skills you can add to your own library toolkit. Let the catalog lead your users to the materials you have carefully selected for them.

We hope that this new edition of *Cataloging Correctly for Kids* will be of service to you in your mission to ignite the curiosity and joy that resides in your users.

Library services and library catalogs have become even more important during times of shelter-in-place and work-from-home. If a library is closed to patrons, there is no physical browsing of the collection. The online catalog is the only way to know what a library owns and the only way to request materials for circulation. All librarians need to know more about how material is cataloged in order to use the online catalog successfully.

I would like to thank all the contributors. A special thanks to the Cataloging of Children's Materials Committee, a long-standing committee of the American Library Association. For many years, this group of librarians championed the specific cataloging needs of children's materials on the international cataloging stage. The committee is also responsible for promoting and producing all editions of *Cataloging Correctly for Kids*.

Thank you to Joanna Fountain and Marilyn McCroskey for their masterful editorial skills and their uncanny ability to keep me focused and inspired during this project.

—**MICHELE ZWIERSKI**, FALL 2020

COPY CATALOGING CORRECTLY

TRINA SODERQUIST | Librarian, Literature Section
U.S. Programs, Law, and Literature Division
Acquisitions and Bibliographic Access Directorate
The Library of Congress

Copy cataloging is the process of adapting another library's existing bibliographic record for local use. It is considered to be more cost-effective and requires less training than original cataloging. However, copy cataloging requires the knowledge of the following:

- where to find bibliographic records to copy or adapt
- how to search for specific records
- how to match bibliographic records against the resource in hand
- how to import or download these records into the local library management system and determine that they have loaded properly
- how to edit bibliographic records according to current cataloging rules and with local practices in mind
- how to add holdings and item information in the local library management system

This chapter will cover all the above except for procedures that require specific knowledge of a local library management system. We cannot explore every scenario for the various local setups of library management systems, bibliographic utilities, vendor interfaces, internet connections, and computer hardware, so where the information in this chapter is too general, we recommend seeking out the assistance of colleagues, vendor representatives, systems administrators, or IT professionals, or searching the internet for support.

SOURCES OF BIBLIOGRAPHIC RECORDS

Bibliographic records can be found in many places on the internet and on the title page verso of many printed books. However, a viewable record is not necessarily a downloadable record, especially if one does not have access—usually by subscription—to the database. Nonetheless, bibliographic information that is only viewable is still useful to a resourceful cataloger. The following is a list of sources for bibliographic records.

Shared catalogs. When a library shares its integrated library management system with other libraries—perhaps as part of a consortium, school district, or public library system—and finds a bibliographic record in the shared catalog that matches the resource in hand, the member library can attach its holding and item information to the communal bibliographic record.

The Library of Congress (LC). The catalog of the Library of Congress (https://catalog.loc.gov) is freely available online. Bibliographic records may be displayed with MARC tags, saved in text or MARC 21 format, downloaded in MARCXML or MODS formats, or exported using the Z39.50 protocol by following instructions on the LC website. It is important to remember that although LC is the de facto national library of the United States, it does not necessarily collect all juvenile or curricular material found in school, public, or curriculum libraries. Within LC, the Children's and Young Adults' Cataloging (CYAC) Program (previously the Annotated Card or AC Program) assigns LC's children's subject headings to juvenile fiction. Most juvenile nonfiction is no longer under its purview and is cataloged in other sections.

CIP data. Another source of copy cataloging, also from LC, is the cataloging-in-publication (CIP) information that is usually printed on the verso of a book's title page. Printed CIP information resembled a catalog card until 2015, when the CIP data block was redesigned to include labels and to accommodate both print and electronic resource data elements. CIP information, which should also be available in LC's online catalog, can be manually entered into a local database. Because CIP data is created before a book is published, it might contain incorrect information (e.g., if the title changes) or incomplete information (because full publication information and pagination are usually unknown until publication).

Bibliographic utilities. OCLC (https://www.oclc.org/en/cataloging-subscription.html), SkyRiver (www.theskyriver.com), and BookWhere (www.bookwhere.net) are examples of fee-based bibliographic utilities. By subscribing to a bibliographic utility, a member library can export bibliographic records directly to its local catalog. WorldCat (https://www.worldcat.org) allows users to search OCLC's database and view or copy from records freely, although bibliographic records cannot be downloaded without an OCLC membership. These bibliographic records are especially useful for verifying or finding details while working with resources.

Outsourcing. In addition to providing access to high-quality records from many sources, including LC, vendors of MARC records may offer other services, such as authority control and labeling. Vendors that offer database services but do not provide the library resources themselves include Backstage Library Works, the Donohue Group, LAC Group, Marcive, and TLC (The Library Corporation). Many distributors, publishers, and book jobbers also provide MARC bibliographic records when libraries make purchases, but the cataloging quality depends on the source of the records. If a library decides to outsource its cataloging, it is still necessary to review the imported bibliographic records and to communicate with the vendors about the sources for its records as well as the library's requirements. Are both LC's *Children's Subject Headings* and Sears headings required? Is Dewey classification mandatory? Does the vendor follow the most current cataloging standards (Resource Description and Access, or RDA)? Are full or minimal records preferred?

Internet-accessible library catalogs. Every online, publicly accessible library catalog is a possible source of copy cataloging. One strategy for finding suitable copy cataloging records is to find a library with a similar collection, such as another school or a curriculum library at a university, and then use its records as the basis for bibliographic records in the local library management system. While searching other library catalogs, it will become clear which libraries provide reliable, relevant cataloging. Even though records cannot be directly exported from these publicly available catalogs, the data is still visible and may be copied and pasted into a local bibliographic record.

SEARCHING FOR BIBLIOGRAPHIC RECORDS

After finding a good source of bibliographic records for copy cataloging, it is necessary to learn to navigate its interface to find the best match for the resource in hand. Help pages always have tips for improving searches and directions for using wildcards, truncation, and Boolean operators. Some database search engines ignore punctuation, including hyphens in ISBNs (International Standard Book Numbers), LCCNs (Library of Congress Control Numbers), and periods in acronyms and abbreviations. While the default keyword search may be adequate for most searches, at other times an advanced search or browsing (or left-anchored searches) is more effective.

Searching for numbers—ISBNs and LCCNs, specifically—is usually more reliable than searching with terms, but not all resources have ISBNs and LCCNs and not all bibliographic records include them. When searching for nonbook formats, other numbers, such as UPCs (Universal Product Codes) and distributor numbers, may be useful for DVDs, CDs, board games, kits, and similar formats Sometimes when searching for a non-distinctive title, an advanced search, combining an author's name with a series title, for example, will be most effective. In addition, qualifiers or facets may be used to limit search results by format, publication date, and so forth.

MATCHING RECORDS WITH RESOURCES

Regardless of the specific search method used, it is necessary to determine whether the search results match the resource in hand by consulting a list of match criteria. Many libraries and consortiums have match criteria documentation, but if not, guidelines developed by others may be searched out and adopted. Ideally, a local copy of all policies, including match criteria documentation, is retained for future staff and to promote consistency within the catalog.

Two examples of match criteria documentation that may be adapted for local use are LC's *Copy Cataloging Manual* and OCLC's "When to Input a New Record." The former is a section of LC's *Descriptive Cataloging Manual* (DCM), which is available by subscription to the web-based service Cataloger's Desktop. This section of the DCM contains LC's procedures for selecting, importing, reviewing, and editing copy cataloging records. Some of the material is specific to LC's database, but many of the checklists can be adapted for local use.

Unlike LC's *Copy Cataloging Manual,* which is only available to those with a paid subscription to Cataloger's Desktop, "When to Input a New Record" is freely available online as a chapter in OCLC's online support document *Bibliographic Formats and Standards.* "When to Input a New Record" provides information to help catalogers determine when to use an existing OCLC record and when to input a new record into OCLC's database. The document addresses each MARC field, explaining whether the absence or presence of the field or differences between fields justifies the creation of a new record.

Even libraries that are not OCLC members may find this document useful as they develop their own match criteria.

Search the internet for more examples of match criteria documentation. Many libraries post documents outlining their technical services procedures. The Duke University Libraries has online copy cataloging documentation that nicely summarizes copy cataloging match criteria, stating that the bibliographic record must match the resource in form, content, and publisher. This involves the following MARC fields and subfields:

- Type of record (LDR/06)
- Title and statement of responsibility (245)
- Edition statement (250)
- Name of publisher (260 $b or 264 $b) and Date of publication (260 $c or 264 $c)
- Extent (300 $a)
- Series statement (490)

Numeric identifiers such as ISBNs, UPCs, or distributor numbers can easily be included on this brief list, because, as noted before, they often provide reliable search results. In fact, the table at the end of this chapter, although presented as a list of MARC fields that need to be reviewed when checking and editing copy cataloging records, may also be used as the basis for creating match criteria documentation.

As the aforementioned Duke document points out, it might not be possible to match a bibliographic record and title page of a resource exactly because cataloging rules have changed over time. Under the earlier Anglo-American Cataloguing Rules (AACR2), catalogers transcribed "first edition" as "1st ed." and "Dr. Ruth K. Westheimer" as "Ruth K. Westheimer." Currently, RDA instructs catalogers to transcribe information from various sources on the resource as it appears, although many catalogers still follow AACR2 practices for title capitalization and transcribing the statement of responsibility. Figure 1.1 is a brief, incomplete listing of some of the more noticeable changes between bibliographic records cataloged under AACR2 versus RDA.

Generally speaking, bibliographic records created using the cataloging standards established in RDA—which was released in 2010 but not widely implemented until 2013—are preferred over earlier records. RDA records should have a MARC field 040 $e rda. Also, full records save time in the cataloging process because incomplete records require more editing. In records used for copy cataloging, if the Encoding Level (LDR/17, or character position 17 of the Leader field) is blank, then the record is fully cataloged. Two other commonly used codes are "3" for abbreviated level and "8" for pre-publication level. While abbreviated level records are usually created by publishers

FIGURE 1.1 | **AACR2 versus RDA: Examples**

Under AACR2	Under RDA
Presence of cataloger-supplied abbreviations	Do not supply abbreviations; do not abbreviate unless the abbreviation appears on the resource; transcribe what is seen
Application of more bracketed (cataloger-supplied or presumed) data	More sources of information are valid, so there is less bracketed data
Practice of "rule of three" limit for names in the statement of responsibility	Record all names in the statement of responsibility (this may affect MARC 100 and 700 fields)
Record publication data in MARC 260 field	Record publication data in MARC 264 field

or vendors, pre-publication (or CIP) level records originate from the Cataloging-in-Publication Program at the Library of Congress. Both types of bibliographic records are produced before the resource is published, so some MARC fields are incomplete or inaccurate. These records need to be edited once they are imported into the local library management system.

When looking for a bibliographic record to match the resource in hand, it is also important to be aware of different cataloging styles or preferences. A good example of this is the various ways to treat books published in a series. Series titles are important in juvenile fiction and nonfiction and in graphic novels.

Mike Maihack's graphic novel series *Cleopatra in Space* has five volumes so far, with separate titles for each individual volume. Bibliographic records for volume #2, *The Thief and the Sword*, can appear several different ways, as shown in these abbreviated bibliographic records:

Record 1

    245 10 $a Cleopatra in space. $n Book two, $p The thief in space / $c Mike Maihack.
    246 30 $a Thief in space
    264 #1 $a New York, NY : $b Graphix, an imprint of Scholastic, $c 2015.
    300 ## $a 187 pages : $b chiefly color illustrations ; $c 24 cm.

Record 2

    245 14 $a The thief in space / $c Mike Maihack.
    264 #1 $a New York, NY : $b Graphix, an imprint of Scholastic, $c 2015.
    300 ## $a 187 pages : $b chiefly color illustrations ; $c 24 cm.
    490 0# $a Cleopatra in space ; $v book two

Record 3

```
245  10  $a Cleopatra in space / $c Mike Maihack.
264  #1  $a New York, NY : $b Graphix, an imprint of Scholastic, $c 2014-
300  ##  $a volumes : $b chiefly color illustrations ; $c 24 cm.
505  1#  $a Book one. Target practice -- Book two. The thief in space -- Book
         three. Secret of the time tablets -- Book four. The golden lion -- Book
         five. Fallen empires
700  12  $a Maihack, Mike. $t Target practice.
700  12  $a Maihack, Mike. $t Thief in space.
700  12  $a Maihack, Mike. $t Secret of the time tablets.
700  12  $a Maihack, Mike. $t Golden lion.
700  12  $a Maihack, Mike. $t Fallen empires.
```

The first two abbreviated records are for the individual volume *The Thief in Space*, whereas the third is for the whole series *Cleopatra in Space*. The first record has the series title as the primary title, while the individual volume title is in MARC field 245 $p and repeated in MARC field 246. (The first indicator "3" of MARC field 246 ensures that the individual volume title *The Thief in Space* is in the database's title index and allows for left-anchored browse title searching.) In the second record, because the individual volume title is in MARC field 245, the series title is in MARC field 490, along with the volume designation "book two." Because the first two records are for *The Thief in Space*, the publication information in MARC field 264 and physical description in MARC field 300 describe that individual volume.

The third record, however, encompasses the whole series, which is not yet complete. Therefore, the publication date in MARC field 264 $c is left open, the physical description in MARC field 300 $a simply says "volumes," the contents note in MARC field 505 is incomplete and does not end in a period, and there are multiple MARC 700 fields for the individual titles (to provide access to the individual titles in the library database's title index).

Which record is the best match for the resource in hand? In this case, all three records are a match for the resource *The Thief and the Sword*, but the better question is, which record is best for an individual library and collection? Which record will work best for librarians or patrons searching for titles in the catalog? Which record will work best for placing holds on individual titles or requesting items? If a library catalog contains the third bibliographic record, depending on the library management system, it may be harder for patrons to determine whether the library has an individual volume and place a hold on it. Because the third record collects all the individual volumes of *Cleopatra in Space* on one record, a patron will need to look at the holdings and item records to see the availability of individual titles. While it may be easier for the cataloger to load a single record for the series and then add volumes as they are published, it may not be the best solution for patrons searching for individual titles in the series.

If a library already has a policy about cataloging series titles, then the choice of bibliographic record is simple. It will be harder if there is no written policy and all three types of records are already in the local catalog. Whatever decision is made, it is important to record it in a local policy document for the benefit of future staff.

ACQUIRING BIBLIOGRAPHIC RECORDS

If a library is part of a school district, library consortium, or public library system, then many of its copy cataloging records will likely come from a shared database. After searching for, matching, and selecting a bibliographic record from the database, one can add the local library's holdings information to the bibliographic record and then add the item for the resource in hand to the holdings record.

Libraries that are members of a bibliographic utility such as OCLC, Sky-River, or BookWhere follow a similar process for locating bibliographic records and then importing them into their local library management systems.

As described earlier, sometimes one has to search other library catalogs to find a bibliographic record to match the resource in hand. If the cataloging module of one's library management system has the capability, or if one has access to Z39.50 software, one can search other libraries' online catalogs for copy cataloging records. The Z39.50 protocol is an international standard that allows for the search and retrieval of information from databases. Z39.50 software may be integrated into the library management system, allowing for searching OCLC or other library catalogs without leaving the local cataloging module interface. The software retrieves records from the external database and imports the bibliographic record into the local library management system for editing.

Separate Z39.50 client software is also available. Often settings can be adjusted or macros can be created so that search results from particular databases are prioritized, and preference is given to full records when importing records. For a list of free and commercial software and for more information about the Z39.50 standard, see the Library of Congress Network Development and MARC Standard Office's web page on Z39.50 (https://www.loc.gov/z3950/agency/).

Finally, copying and pasting can be a good solution if a different edition (e.g., the large-print version) of a resource is already in the local catalog. Some consider this to be a form of copy cataloging, but in this instance a new bibliographic record is being created to match the item in hand.

EDITING BIBLIOGRAPHIC RECORDS

After importing bibliographic records into the local library management system, it is necessary to review and edit them. At the very least, it is important to make sure the correct record is downloaded and that a duplicate record is not imported or the wrong record is replaced. Uncorrected errors in copy cataloging can generate problems, including duplication of orders, the inability to find materials, and patron frustration. A patron might search the catalog for a fairy tale illustrated by a beloved artist, only to go to the shelf and discover a book with a different illustrator because the wrong record was linked to the library's resource. Or, what if someone requires a large-print book, but the library's copies cannot be found because large-print copies were added to the bibliographic record for regular-print editions?

In the fifth edition of *Cataloging Correctly for Kids* (2011), Deborah A. Fritz commented that many administrators do not want librarians to spend a lot of time editing records, writing, "Don't let them catch you doing it, but do it just the same." The implication is that, for some administrators, editing copy cataloging records is not an effective use of their librarians' time and effort. In a production-oriented environment where quantity is emphasized, accepting copy cataloging records "as-is" is preferred. Also, if the process is automated and records are batch loaded, then accepting records as-is is more efficient. After all, one of the underlying principles of copy cataloging is the assumption that all catalogers everywhere are following the same standards and are producing satisfactory bibliographic records.

At the same time, some editing is necessary. Section B13.2.1 of LC's *Copy Cataloging Manual* states that "LC copy cataloging focuses on accepting the cataloging of other libraries as much as possible, limiting changes to those judged 'egregious' ('egregious' in this context means data that are inaccurate, misleading, or result in denial of access)." Obvious errors like typos—which cause keyword search failures—should be corrected, and changes should be made to reflect differences in the resource in hand.

It is important to edit copy cataloging records if the modifications enhance the local record for the benefit of the patrons. For example, if the local copy of a resource has a sticker or emblem on the cover, indicating that the title is a Caldecott or Newbery Medal winner, then add a MARC field 586 awards note. Add name or title access entry points if they are missing, especially if they will help patrons find materials. To better serve patrons, it might be necessary to add data to the local record from the record for a different edition. If the local record lacks *Children's Subject Headings* or Sears headings, a Dewey number, or a summary, one can search other bibliographic records for the missing information and add it to the local record.

As mentioned earlier, brief records created by vendors and pre-publication level records will need editing. At the very least, the physical description of the item will need to be added to the MARC 300 field. When searching for a misshelved book, it is helpful to know that it has 32 pages and is 28 cm tall, rather than 326 pages and 20 cm tall.

Libraries need to create and maintain documentation or a checklist for copy cataloging procedures, especially if there is a specialized collection or patron base that requires the application of many local policies. Figure 1.2

FIGURE 1.2 | **Common MARC fields to review when copy cataloging**

Name (OCLC Mnemonic)	MARC Field	Action
Type of record (Type)	LDR/06	Check that the code matches the description given in 300 $a and the resource in hand. This field often generates the material type icon in OPACs. See *MARC 21 Format for Bibliographic Data for codes.*
Encoding level (ELvl)	LDR/17	Check for completeness of cataloging: blank for fully cataloged, "3" for abbreviated level, and "8" for prepublication level. *See MARC 21 Format for Bibliographic Data* for more codes.
Descriptive cataloging form (Desc)	LDR/18	Check for "i" (ISBD) for RDA records. Earlier records cataloged under AACR2 will be coded "a."
Type of date (DtSt)	008/06	Check that the code reflects the type of date in 264 (260 in AACR2 records).
Date 1 and Date 2 (Dates)	008/ 07-14	Check that the date(s) is (are) correct and agree with date(s) provided in 264 (or 260).
Place of publication (Ctry)	008/ 15-17	Check that the code reflects the place of publication on the resource and matches 264 (or 260) $a. See the MARC Code List for Countries (https://www.loc.gov/marc/countries/).
Target audience (Audn)	008/22	For juvenile material, check that the code is "j." Other codes for children's materials are "a," "b," "c," and "d" for specific age and grade ranges.
Language (Lang)	008/ 35-37	Check that the code matches the language of the resource. See MARC Code List for Languages (https://www.loc.gov/marc/languages/).
ISBN	020	Check that the ISBN number matches the resource. This is important for distinguishing between editions.

Name (OCLC Mnemonic)	MARC Field	Action
Cataloging source	040	Check for $b eng for English-language cataloging records and $e rda for RDA cataloging. Check for "DLC" (Library of Congress) or another trusted source for records. See the MARC Code List for Organizations (https://www.loc.gov/marc/organizations/).
Authentication code	042	Check for "lc" (Library of Congress), "lcac" (LC CYAC Program), "lccopycat" (LC Copy Cataloging), or "pcc" (Program for Cooperative Cataloging). See the MARC Authentication Action Code List (https://www.loc.gov/standards/valuelist/marcauthen.html).
Library of Congress call number	050	Check that the call number fits into the local shelflist (if LC Classification is used).
Dewey Decimal classification number	082	Check for the presence of the Dewey number if the library uses Dewey Classification.
Main entry fields (Primary access points in RDA)	1xx	Check that the information matches the resource.
Title statement	245	Check that indicators are correct. The first indicator specifies whether a title added entry is made. A first indicator of "1" shows that a 1xx main entry is present and the title is indexed. A first indicator of "0" is used when the title is the primary access point or main entry. The second indicator specifies the number of characters that should be skipped in filing. For example, if the title begins with the article "an," then the indicator should be "3" (two characters, one for each letter, and one character for the space).
Varying form of title	246	Add if needed or useful for increased access.
Edition statement	250	Check that the information matches the resource.
Production, publication, distribution, manufacture, and copyright notice	264 (260 in AACR2 records)	Check that the information matches the resource.
Physical description	300	Check that the information matches the resource. Check for "illustrations" in $b if the resource is intended for children and has illustrations.
Content type	336	For print monographs, check for $a text $2 rdacontent.
Media type	337	For print monographs, check for $a unmediated $2 rdamedia.
Carrier type	338	For print monographs, check for $a volume $2 rdacarrier.
Series statement	490	Check that the information matches the resource. Series are often searched for and followed by avid child readers.

Name (OCLC Mnemonic)	MARC Field	Action
Summary, etc.	520	Check or supply if the resource is intended for children. Remember that this note also supplies terms for keyword searching.
Formatted contents note	505	Add chapter headings—especially for collections of literature—if needed or useful for increased access.
Subject access fields	6xx	Check the second indicator, which shows the source of the subject heading: "0" for LC Subject Headings, "1" for LC Children's Subject Headings, and "7" (or "8" in some databases) with "$2 sears" for Sears headings.
Added entry fields (Secondary access points in RDA)	7xx	Check or add access points for illustrators if the resource is intended for children. Add other contributors if needed or useful for increased access.
Series added entry	8xx	Check that the information matches authorized form found in authority files. Note that LC stopped creating and updating series authority records in 2006.

shows some of the MARC fields to review when checking and editing copy cataloging records. Note that the presence or absence of the following MARC fields, or differing data in the fields, does not mean a bibliographic record is not a match for the resource in hand. As mentioned before when discussing match criteria documentation, the critical fields are Type of record (MARC LDR/06), Title statement (MARC 245), Edition statement (MARC 250), Publication information (MARC 260 or 264), Physical description (MARC 300), and Series statement (MARC 490). Not all bibliographic records will have or need all of the MARC fields above.

CONCLUSION

Copy cataloging can be as simple or as intricate as desired, depending on available time, knowledge, and inclination. But regardless of whether one's library is production-oriented, focusing on accepting as much copy cataloging as possible, or it wants to make sure every call number and subject heading is correct, it is most important for libraries to create and maintain documentation of their copy cataloging practices to maintain consistency in their local catalogs. What are the criteria for matching copy cataloging records to the resources in hand? What MARC fields need to be checked or added to improve accessibility? How can bibliographic records best help patrons?

RESOURCES

Duke University Libraries. "Copy Cataloging." In *Monographic Cataloging Policies and Procedures.* https://library.duke.edu/about/depts/cataloging/documentation/copy-cataloging.

Fritz, Deborah A. "Copy Cataloging Correctly." In *Cataloging Correctly for Kids: An Introduction to the Tools,* 5th ed., edited by Sheila S. Intner, Joanna F. Fountain, and Jean Weihs, 49-72. Chicago: American Library Association, 2011.

Library of Congress. *Copy Cataloging Manual.* See Cataloger's Desktop home page. https://www.loc.gov/cds/desktop/.

———. *Descriptive Cataloging Manual.* See Cataloger's Desktop home page. https://www.loc.gov/cds/desktop/.

———. *Library of Congress Catalog.* catalog.loc.gov.

———. "When to Input a New Record." *Descriptive Cataloging Manual.*

Library of Congress, Network Development and MARC Standards Office. *MARC 21 Format for Bibliographic Data.* 1999 edition, update no. 1 (October 2000) through update no. 27 (November 2018). www.loc.gov/marc/bibliographic/.

———. *MARC Code List for Countries.* 2003 edition, last updated April 4, 2008. www.loc.gov/marc/countries/.

———. *MARC Code List for Languages.* 2007 edition, updated continuously. www.loc.gov/marc/languages/.

———. *MARC Code List for Relators.* May 9, 2016. www.loc.gov/marc/relators/.

———. *Term and Code List for RDA Carrier Types.* March 25, 2016. www.loc.gov/standards/valuelist/rdacarrier.html.

———. *Term and Code List for RDA Content Types.* April 5, 2011. www.loc.gov/standards/valuelist/rdacontent.html.

———. *Term and Code List for RDA Media Types.* April 5, 2011. www.loc.gov/standards/valuelist/rdamedia.html.

———. *Z39.50.* Updated November 2015. www.loc.gov/z3950/agency/.

OCLC WorldCat Quality Management Division, *Bibliographic Formats and Standards.* Fourth edition. www.oclc.org/bibformats/en.html.

RDA Steering Committee. *RDA: Resource Description and Access.* Chicago: American Library Association; Ottawa: Canadian Federation of Library Associations; London: Chartered Institute of Library and Information Professionals (CILIP), 2010- .

———. *RDA Toolkit.* https://www.rdatoolkit.org/.

2

HOW THE CATALOGING IN PUBLICATION (CIP) PROGRAM HELPS CHILDREN'S LIBRARIANS

CAROLINE SACCUCCI | Chief
U.S. Programs, Law, and Literature Division, Acquisitions and Bibliographic
Access Directorate
The Library of Congress

The Cataloging in Publication (CIP) program is a national program of the Library of Congress (LC). Begun in 1971, its mission is to provide catalog records in advance of publication as a service to the nation's libraries. The CIP program works directly with U.S. publishers to receive galleys or key information about their forthcoming titles to create the pre-publication cataloging or metadata. The CIP program serves as both a metadata creation program for U.S. forthcoming titles and a source of new acquisitions for the Library's collections. Publishers send pre-publication information for forthcoming books to LC by logging into PrePub Book Link (www.loc.gov/publish/prepubbook link/), an online CIP data request portal. The cataloging data block, prepared in advance of publication, is printed in the book; complete bibliographic records can be distributed to bibliographic utilities as well as to publishers and vendors. Today approximately 2,500 publishers participate in the CIP program.

The CIP program attempts to cover materials that are likely to be collected by most libraries in the United States—primarily English-language books, but also books in Western European languages as well as many bilingual English-Spanish books. Certain materials are not eligible for the CIP program, including:

- textbooks below the secondary level
- consumable materials (e.g., those meant to be cut out or written in, such as workbooks)
- ephemeral or consumable materials (e.g., calendars and phone books)
- "tie-ins" (to television, movies, etc.), music scores, and mass-market publications
- phonics books
- audiovisual materials

For a complete list of exclusions with explanations, refer to the list of ineligible categories of material (www.loc.gov/publish/cip/about/ineligible.html) on the CIP web page. Even with these exclusions, CIP data is created for a significant percentage of monographs published in the United States, including a large number of juvenile trade books.

PROGRAM DESCRIPTION

Publishers who wish to participate in the CIP program apply though PrePub Book Link. They need to indicate that they have published at least three titles by three different authors, and that a WorldCat search shows that these three titles are widely acquired by U.S. libraries. Once accepted into the CIP program, participating publishers submit an application for each title and attach an electronic galley to each submission. The application data is converted to MARC data and catalogers review the MARC fields, updating as necessary to reflect the galley. After catalogers complete the cataloging, PrePub Book Link sends the publisher a link to the complete CIP data block. The publisher prints the CIP data block in its entirety in the book, usually on the verso of the title page but sometimes on the last pages.

The CIP data block printed in the book has appeared in a labeled format since 2015. The CIP labels with their data elements are as follows:

- Names: authors, editors, illustrators, etc.
- Title: book title, subtitle, and statement(s) of responsibility
- Other titles: preferred (uniform) title, variant forms of title, parallel title, etc.
- Description: publisher name, publisher place, and publication date; series title(s), audience level, notes, and summary

Instructions for Downloading a MARC Record from the Library of Congress Catalog

The CIP data block provides the LCCN permalink, or persistent URL, as the last line of text. The LC record shown in figure 2.1 is available at https://lccn.loc .gov/2018056157.

FIGURE 2.1 | **CIP data block**

```
Library of Congress Cataloging-in-Publication Data

Names: Berne, Emma Carlson, author. | Palin, Tim, illustrator. | Mallman, Mark,
    composer.
Title: The days of the week / by Emma Carlson Berne ; illustrated by Tim
    Palin ; music by Mark Mallman.
Description: North Mankato, MN ; Cantata Learning, 2020. | Series: Patterns of
    time | Includes bibliographical references. | Audience: K to Grade 3.|
    Audience: Ages 3-6.
Identifiers: LCCN 2018053644 | ISBN 9781684104086 (hardcover)
Subjects: LCSH: Days--Juvenile literature. | Calendars--Juvenile literature.
Classification: LCC CE13 .B47 2020 | DDC    529/.1--dc23
LC record available at https://lccn.loc.gov/2018053644
```

You can either search for a particular record using the LCCN permalink in a CIP data block or search the catalog for the record.

To download a MARC record from the Library of Congress catalog, select the Save Record option from the list found on the right-hand side of the page showing the record.

You will be given a choice via drop-down list to save the record in MARC (Unicode/UTF-8) or MARC (Non-Unicode/MARC-8). Select MARC (Unicode/UTF-8) and click Save.

Once you have saved the record, your browser will prompt you to save the file to your computer as a Notepad (.mrc) file. The LC catalog export file is always named "records.mrc," so you will need to change the file name. Make sure to give the record a meaningful file name, such as the LCCN, ISBN, or even a brief version of author's name or the title. At this point, the record is saved as a text file on your PC, not in your catalog.

Depending on your cataloging client, you may need to choose **Import** the Record File or simply **Open** the Record File to bring up the record and save it to your local catalog.

- Identifiers: Library of Congress Control Number (LCCN) (print), LCCN (e-book), and the International Standard Book Numbers [ISBN(s)] associated with print and e-book versions
- Subjects: *Library of Congress Subject Headings* (LCSH) for adults, *Library of Congress Children's and Young Adults' Subject Headings* (CYAC) for juvenile fiction, Sears headings for *selected* juvenile nonfiction, genre/form terms, and Book Industry Standards and Communications (BISAC) headings
- Classification: *Library of Congress Classification* (LCC) and Dewey Decimal Classification (DDC)
- LCCN permalink

In addition to the CIP data printed in books, an electronic (MARC) version of the CIP data is created. These MARC records are available for free download from LC's online catalog (https://catalog.loc.gov/) or can be purchased in batches with a weekly subscription by contacting the Cataloging Distribution Service (www.loc.gov/cds/). Large libraries, bibliographic utilities, commercial cataloging services, and book wholesalers often subscribe. In turn, they make the records available to their customers or users.

Because CIP records are available before the book is published, publishers and wholesalers can use CIP records to advertise forthcoming materials. Libraries receiving CIP data can preorder and publicize these new materials to their users.

Some CIP data may have changed since publication because the book was cataloged quite early in the pre-publication stage. There are frequent changes to the title, order of authors, and other data. It is important to compare the CIP data with the title page and other sources in the book itself so that local cataloging data accurately represent the material in hand. While the CIP record should be treated as high-quality cataloging, it will lack some data elements and may need to be updated to reflect the published item.

CIP AND LOCAL CATALOGING

When material arrives in a library, a catalog record must be created before access and circulation can take place. If a relatively new book contains CIP data, quality cataloging already exists, and a librarian needs only to capture that record for local use. Books published without CIP data require that someone on the library's staff produce the cataloging, look for another library's cataloging to copy, or set the item aside to wait for cataloging to appear in whatever sources the library uses. Books with CIP data can go on the library shelf sooner. Some books are published without CIP data or with only the LCCN, so it is important to search first to see if a cataloging record does exist for that title.

When cataloging data is available, librarians with an online catalog have a few options for taking advantage of this. MARC records may be available through a publisher, a bibliographic utility, or a commercial provider. Libraries belonging to a bibliographic utility will find MARC available to be exported. MARC records are also available for free download from the LC catalog. (See page 17 for instructions for downloading instructions.) In short, no matter how a library builds its catalog, the CIP program can save it time and money.

Figures 2.2 and 2.3 illustrate how the CIP data block maps to a labeled cataloging input screen or labeled record display. Local libraries can use the CIP data to build a record. Elements may be omitted or repeated (e.g., for

FIGURE 2.2 | **Actual: CIP series, audience level, and notes data mapped to local interface**

```
Library of Congress Cataloging-in-Publication Data

Names: Berne, Emma Carlson, author. | Palin, Tim, illustrator. | Mallman, Mark,
    composer.
Title: The days of the week / by Emma Carlson Berne ; illustrated by Tim
    Palin ; music by Mark Mallman.
Description: North Mankato, MN : Cantata Learning, 2020. | Series: Patterns of
    time | Includes bibliographical references. | Audience: K to Grade 3. |
    Audience: Ages 3-6.
Identifiers: LCCN 2018053644 | ISBN 9781684104086 (hardcover)
Subjects: LCSH: Days--Juvenile literature. | Calendars--Juvenile literature.
Classification: LCC CE13 .B47 2020 | DDC    529/.1--dc23
LC record available at https://lccn.loc.gov/2018053644
```

	Cataloging Input Screen or Labeled Display
Author(s), illustrator(s), etc.	Berne, Emma Carlson, author.
Author(s), illustrator(s), etc.	Palin, Tim, illustrator.
Author(s), illustrator(s), etc.	Mallman, Mark, composer.
Title / Statement of Responsibility	The days of the week / by Emma Carlson, Berne; illustrated by Tim Palin ; music by Mark Mallman.
Location	North Mankato, MN
Publisher	Cantata Learning
Publication Date	2020
Series	Patterns of time
Notes	Includes bibliographical references and index
Audience	K to Grade 3
Audience	Ages 3-6
LCCN	2018053644
ISBN	9781684104086 (hardcover)
LC Subject Heading	Days—Juvenile literature
LC Subject Heading	Calendars—Juvenile literature
Dewey Classification	529/.1—[ed.]23
LC Record	https://lccn.loc.gov/2018053644

multiple subjects) depending on your local system or local needs. Figure 2.2 includes series, audience level, and notes. Figure 2.3 includes summary, CYAC children's and young adult subject headings, and BISAC terms. Both examples show other types of elements typically found in CIP records.

FIGURE 2.3 | **Summary, CYAC** *Children's and Young Adult Subject Headings* **and BISAC terms mapped to local interface**

```
Library of Congress Cataloging-in-Publication Data

Names: Lennon, John, 1940-1980, author. | McCartney, Paul, author. |
   Rosenthal, Marc, 1949- illustrator.
Title: All you need is love / written by John Lennon and Paul McCartney ;
   illustrated by Marc Rosenthal.
Description: First Little Simon hardcover edition. | New York : Little Simon,
   2019. | Audience: Ages 4-8. | Summary: Illustrations and easy-to-read text
   share John Lennon and Paul McCartney's world-renowned song that celebrates
   the love that surrounds us.
Identifiers: LCCN 2018033372| ISBN 9781534429819 (hardback) | ISBN
   9781534429826 (ebook)
Subjects: LCSH: Children's songs, English--England--Texts. | CYAC:
   Love--Songs and music. | Songs. | BISAC: JUVENILE FICTION / Love &
   Romance. | JUVENILE FICTION / Performing Arts / Music. | JUVENILE FICTION
   / Social Issues / Emotions & Feelings.
Classification: LCC PS8.3.L5399 A1 2019 | DDC 782.42 [E] --dc23
LC record available at https://lccn.loc.gov/2018033372L
```

	Cataloging Input Screen or Labeled Display
Author(s), illustrator(s), etc.	Lennon, John, 1940-1980, author.
Author(s), illustrator(s), etc.	McCartney, Paul, author.
Author(s), illustrator(s), etc.	Rosenthal, Marc, 1949- , illustrator.
Title / Statement of Responsibility	All you need is love / by John Lennon, and Paul McCartney ; illustrated by Marc Rosenthal.
Edition	First Little Simon hardcover edition.
Location	New York
Publisher	Little Simon
Publication Date	2019
Summary	Illustrations and easy-to-read text...
LCCN	2018033372
ISBN	978153442819 (hardcover)
LC Subject Heading	Days--Juvenile literature
Children's Subject Heading	Love—Songs and music.
BISAC Term	JUVENILE FICTION / Love & Romance
Dewey Classification	782.421—[ed.]23
LC Record	https://lccn.loc.gov/2018033372

Figures 2.4 and 2.5 display how the same CIP data presented in Figures 2.2 and 2.3 map to the corresponding MARC-tagged record found in the LC Catalog. As shown in these figures, the labels found in the CIP data block refer to the major groupings of elements contained in the MARC record. The box to the right of the record lists the relevant MARC tags.

FIGURE 2.4 | **CIP data mapped to fields in a MARC record**

```
Library of Congress Cataloging-in-Publication Data

Names: Berne, Emma Carlson, author. | Palin, Tim, illustrator. | Mallman, Mark,
    composer.
Title: The days of the week / by Emma Carlson Berne ; illustrated by Tim
    Palin ; music by Mark Mallman.
Description: North Mankato, MN : Cantata Learning, 2020. | Series: Patterns of
    time | Includes bibliographical references. | Audience: K to Grade 3.|
    Audience: Ages 3-6.
Identifiers: LCCN 2018053644 | ISBN 9781684104086 (hardcover)
Subjects: LCSH: Days--Juvenile literature. | Calendars--Juvenile literature.
Classification: LCC CE13 .B47 2020 | DDC    529/.1--dc23
LC record available at https://lccn.loc.gov/2018053644
```

MARC Tagged Record

```
010 __ |a 2018053644
020 __ |a 9781684104086 (hardcover)
040 __ |a DLC |b eng |c DLC |e rda |d DLC
042 __ |a pcc
050 00 |a CE13 |b .B47 2020
082 00 |a 529/.1 |2 23
100 1_ |a Berne, Emma Carlson, |e author.
245 14 |a The days of the week / |c by Emma Carlson Berne ;
        illustrated by Tim Palin ; music by Mark Mallman.
264 _1 |a North Mankato, MN : |b Cantata Learning, |c [2020]
300 __ |a pages cm.
336 __ |a text |b txt |2 rdacontent
337 __ |a unmediated |b n |2 rdamedia
338 __ |a volume |b nc |2 rdacarrier
490 0_ |a Patterns of time
504 __ |a Includes bibliographical references.
521 __ |a K to Grade 3.
521 __ |a Ages 3-6.
650 _0 |a Days |v Juvenile literature.
650 _0 |a Calendars |v Juvenile literature.
700 1_ |a Palin, Tim, |e illustrator.
700 1_ |a Mallman, Mark, |e composer.
```

MARC CODES
010 – LCCN
020 – ISBN
050 – LC classification
082 – Dewey class no.
100 – Personal name
245 – Main Title
250 – Edition
264 – Published/Produced
336 – Content type
337 – Media type
338 – Carrier type
490 – Series
504 – Notes
505 – Contents Note
520 – Summary
650 – Subjects

FIGURE 2.5 | **CYAC information from CIP data mapped to fields in a MARC record**

```
Library of Congress Cataloging-in-Publication Data

Names: Lennon, John, 1940-1980, author. | McCartney, Paul, author. |
    Rosenthal, Marc, 1949- illustrator.
Title: All you need is love / written by John Lennon and Paul McCartney ;
    illustrated by Marc Rosenthal.
Description: First Little Simon hardcover edition. | New York : Little Simon,
    2019. | Audience: Ages 4-8. | Summary: Illustrations and easy-to-read text
    share John Lennon and Paul McCartney's world-renowned song that celebrates
    the love that surrounds us.
Identifiers: LCCN 2018033372| ISBN 9781534429819 (hardback) | ISBN
    9781534429826 (ebook)
Subjects: LCSH: Children's songs, English--England--Texts. | CYAC:
    Love--Songs and music. | Songs. | BISAC: JUVENILE FICTION / Love &
    Romance. | JUVENILE FICTION / Performing Arts / Music. | JUVENILE FICTION
    / Social Issues / Emotions & Feelings.
Classification: LCC PS8.3.L5399 A1 2019 | DDC 782.42 [E] --dc23
LC record available at https://lccn.loc.gov/2018033372L
```

MARC Record

```
010 __ |a 2018033372
020 __ |a 9781534429819 (hardback)
040 __ |a DLC |b eng |c DLC |e rda |d DLC
042 __ |a pcc |a lcac
050 00 |a PZ8.3.L5399 |b A1 2019
082 00 |a 782.42 |a E |2 23
100 1_ |a Lennon, John, |d 1940-1980, |e author.
245 10 |a All you need is love / |c written by John Lennon and
        Paul McCartney ; illustrated by Marc Rosenthal.
250 __ |a First Little Simon hardcover edition.
264 _1 |a New York : |b Little Simon, |c 2019.
300 __ |a pages cm
336 __ |a text |b txt |2 rdacontent
336 __ |a still image |b sti |2 rdacontent
337 __ |a unmediated |b n |2 rdamedia
338 __ |a volume |b nc |2 rdacarrier
520 __ |a Illustrations and easy-to-read text share John Lennon and Paul McCartney's
        world-renowned song that celebrates the love that surrounds us.
650 _0 |a Children's songs, English |z England |v Texts.
650 _1 |a Love |v Songs and music.
650 _1 |a Songs.
650 _7 |a JUVENILE FICTION / Love & Romance. |2 bisacsh
650 _7 |a JUVENILE FICTION / Performing Arts / Music. |2 bisacsh
650 _7 |a JUVENILE FICTION / Social Issues / Emotions & Feelings. |2 bisacsh
700 1_ |a McCartney, Paul, |e author.
7001 _ |a Rosenthal, Marc, |d 1949- |e illustrator.
```

MARC CODES
010 – LCCN
020 – ISBN
050 – LC classification
082 – Dewey class no.
100 – Personal name
245 – Main Title
250 – Edition
264 – Published/Produced
336 – Content type
337 – Media type
338 – Carrier type
490 – Series
504 – Notes
520 – Summary
650 – Subjects
776– Links to online record

With the labeled display, libraries with card catalogs may choose to reproduce the data on the card exactly as it appears in the CIP data block. The CIP program no longer uses the card catalog format to display the CIP data.

An important part of the cataloging process is to verify the accuracy of the CIP data. During the publication process, descriptive elements can change, and the record must be corrected in order for the material to be successfully accessed. For example, the exact title or the order of author names may have been changed prior to actual publication. The CIP data block cannot be changed once it has been printed in the book, but the MARC records are verified and updated when the books arrive at LC. Publishers send finished copies of their books to LC for its collections as their final responsibility in the CIP process. It remains the responsibility of the local library, however, to make the appropriate changes or to check for complete and updated records for books for which there are MARC records. Either way, local records based on CIP information should be reviewed with the book in hand. Some libraries choose not to complete the CIP data by adding information missing from the records, such as the physical description portion of the cataloging record (MARC field 300), although the data describing the extent of the item are required as core elements of an RDA record (RDA 3.4.5). (Resource Description and Access, or RDA, is the international cataloging standard that replaced the Anglo-American Cataloguing Rules.)

SERVICE BENEFITS

In addition to the time and resources saved during cataloging, the CIP program provides service benefits. As mentioned, CIP data has potential as a marketing tool for publishers and book wholesalers. Libraries benefit from obtaining high-quality bibliographic information about forthcoming publications before they are received. Also, because the CIP block is printed in the book, anyone holding it can refer to it. Students, teachers, parents, or bookstore browsers can look at this area and find useful information such as annotations or summaries, intended audience notes, reading levels, subject areas, classification, and more at a glance.

CONCLUSION

The CIP program provides pre-publication cataloging for most juvenile trade publications issued in the United States. As such, it is an important information source for children's and young adults' services librarians as well as for catalogers and other librarians and media specialists responsible for producing catalog records for their institutions. Thanks to CIP, materials arriving with cataloging printed inside can be placed on library shelves quickly.

CATALOGING NONBOOK CHILDREN'S MATERIALS

TRINA SODERQUIST | Librarian, Literature Section
U.S. Programs, Law, and Literature Division
Acquisitions and Bibliographic Access Directorate
The Library of Congress

EMILY CREO | Head of Cataloging
Four County Library System
Vestal, New York

Nonbook cataloging is a wide and varied realm, and, perhaps obviously, may be defined as the creation of metadata to represent information resources that are not printed books. Other terms for nonbook cataloging and its aspects include audiovisual cataloging, music cataloging, nonprint cataloging, and special formats cataloging.

For the purposes of this chapter, nonbook cataloging includes many materials commonly collected by public, school, and university K-12 curriculum libraries for their educational, informational, and recreational value—sound and videorecordings, cartographic and graphic materials, electronic resources, and three-dimensional objects.

This is not a comprehensive guide to cataloging nonbook children's materials. Rather, the intent is to present a basic, practical introduction to and reference for identifying copy cataloging records and creating original bibliographic records for nonbook information resources. This chapter does not cover manuscript materials, tactile materials for the visually impaired (or braille materials), music scores, microform, or serials.

WHY CATALOG NONBOOK MATERIALS?

In a 1983 *American Libraries* article describing the results of a survey she administered, Sheila S. Intner argued for the "equality of cataloging." She praised AACR2—then the international standard for cataloging—because it "treat[ed] all media according to a single bibliographic pattern. AACR2 thus offered libraries a chance to integrate the cataloging of media with all other bibliographic records, processes, and displays." Intner encouraged libraries to use AACR2 to catalog their media collections for greater discoverability and accessibility. The same argument can be made today, regardless of whether the bibliographic record is created using AACR2 or RDA, the current cataloging standard. RDA aims to be format-neutral and emphasizes the intellectual content of information resources rather than physical format. Cataloging rules and standards accommodate information resources in many formats so they may easily be integrated into a single catalog.

Even if the logistics of space and shelving or the desire to protect fragile collections prohibit the physical integration of nonbook and book materials in the library, all the library's resources can cohabitate in the integrated library system. This can aid acquisitions processes, as reports are generated to see which subject areas have significant nonbook holdings and which need to be increased. Other reports may be run to identify lost inventory to replace, and the integrated library system can keep account of nonbook expenditures.

As mentioned earlier, cataloging nonbook information resources improves discoverability and accessibility. Children, parents, and schoolteachers will be pleased to find hand puppets to correspond to favorite fairy tales. They will also appreciate easily locating models of the solar system and human body, write-on United States maps, and mathematics manipulatives.

RESOURCES FOR CATALOGING NONBOOK MATERIALS

As with cataloging printed books, the primary resources for cataloging nonbook information resources are AACR2, RDA, and MARC 21. For subject headings, catalogers can use the *Sears List of Subject Headings* or consult the *Library of Congress Subject Headings* and the *Subject Headings Manual,* and classification can be done with Dewey or the *Library of Congress Classification* systems. Alternatively, if nonbook materials are shelved separately from printed books, depending on the size of the collection and whether they are available for general browsing, they could be classed by accession number, by music genre, or alphabetically by artist, composer, or performer.

Of particular interest to nonbook catalogers is the *Library of Congress Genre/Form Term List,* which allows catalogers to apply terms describing what an information resource *is* rather than what it is *about.* Other thesauri, like the OLAC *Video Game Genre Terms* or the *Art & Architecture Thesaurus,* can provide specificity where other ontologies fall short.

Additionally, beginners and seasoned catalogers can find guidance from experts in cataloging the specific type of material. For cataloging videorecordings, streaming media, video games, and more, the guides and best practice recommendations issued by OLAC (Online Audiovisual Catalogers) are highly recommended, as are its biennial conferences and electronic discussion list. The website and electronic discussion list of the Music Library Association (MLA) provide excellent information on cataloging music scores and sound recordings. For cartographic materials, a good starting point is the *Map Cataloger's Tool Box* online. Print resources, even those that are older and address cataloging using AACR2, may be useful, such as Nancy B. Olson's *Cataloging of Audiovisual Materials and Other Special Materials: A Manual Based on AACR2 and MARC 21* (2008).

IDENTIFYING THE TYPE OF RECORD

Whether searching for bibliographic records to use for copy cataloging or creating an original bibliographic record, the first step is to identify the nonbook material according to the definitions provided by AACR2, RDA, and MARC 21. This information is coded in the Leader, which primarily contains system-supplied data elements that provide information to the integrated library system for processing the record, but catalogers are able to select the type of record, which is coded in the LDR/06 byte. Figure 3.1 shows many of the codes relevant to nonbook children's catalogers, along with abbreviated guidelines for what resources fall into each record type.

Sometimes the material in hand falls into more than one type of record category. Information resources issued on CD-ROMs are not automatically assigned an LDR/06 of "m" for computer file. Electronic resources like CD-ROMs and floppy disks are coded according to their most significant aspect. If a PowerPoint presentation on CD-ROM is mostly textual with a few incidental images, then it should be coded "a" for language material. If a CD-ROM contains reproductions of famous paintings, then assign "k" for two-dimensional nonprojectable graphic. Similarly, a three-dimensional globe jigsaw puzzle should be coded "e" for cartographic material.

When a resource has multiple format characteristics, a MARC field 006 is added to account for the computer file aspects of a text or graphic on CD-ROM or for the three-dimensionality of a globe puzzle, as in the previous instances. In these cases, and when cataloging resources have accompanying material

FIGURE 3.1 I **Common codes for nonbook resources**

Code	Description
a—Language material	Used for non-manuscript language material. Includes electronic resources that are basically textual in nature.
e—Cartographic material	Used for non-manuscript cartographic material. Includes maps, atlases, globes, digital maps, and other cartographic items.
g—Projected medium	Used for videorecordings (including digital video), slides, and transparencies. Includes material specifically designed for overhead projection.
i—Nonmusical sound recording	Used for a recording of nonmusical sounds (e.g., speech).
j—Musical sound recording	Used for a musical sound recording (e.g., compact discs or cassette tapes).
k—Two-dimensional nonprojectable graphic	Used for two-dimensional nonprojectable graphics such as activity cards, computer graphics, digital pictures, flash cards, photo CDs, pictures, posters, study prints, and reproductions of any of these.
m—Computer file	Used for the following classes of electronic resources: computer software (including programs, games, and fonts) and online systems or services.
o—Kit	Used for a mixture of various components issued as a unit and intended primarily for instructional purposes where no one item is the predominant component of it. Examples are packages of assorted materials, such as a set of school social studies curriculum material (books, workbooks, guides, activities, etc.) or packages of educational test materials (tests, answer sheets, scoring guides, score charts, interpretative manuals, etc.).
r—Three-dimensional artifact or naturally occurring object	Includes manmade objects such as models, dioramas, games, puzzles, machines, and toys. Also includes naturally occurring objects such as microscope specimens.

in a different format from the primary resource, the MARC 006 field is an extension of the MARC 008 field, character positions 18 through 34. This will be discussed more in a later part of the chapter.

Often the LDR/06 is coded without the cataloger realizing it. When creating original bibliographic records in the cataloging modules of many integrated library systems and bibliographic utilities, the user first selects a template or workform according to the type of material being cataloged. This selection determines the coding of the LDR/06 and the definitions of character positions 18 through 34 in MARC field 008.

It is important to pay attention to the coding in the LDR/06 because it helps in determining the material type icon that displays in online catalogs.

This becomes significant when looking at a title that is available in many formats. Is the patron searching for J. K. Rowling's *Harry Potter and the Chamber of Secrets* as a printed book, as an e-book, as an audiobook on CD, as a video-recording on DVD, or as a video game?

MARC FIELDS IN NONBOOK CATALOGING

Current cataloging standards require the identification of a preferred source of information when cataloging an information resource. For all items, the source for bibliographic data is the material itself, which can include the storage medium (paper, film, plastic, cardboard, etc.); any housing that is an integral part of the resource (a cassette, a cartridge, etc.); a container issued with the resource (a game box, a CD jewel case, a carrying case, etc.); and eye-readable labels permanently printed on or affixed to the resource.

When following AACR2 conventions, any data taken from outside the preferred source of information should be enclosed in brackets and a note must be made naming the outside source. RDA instructs catalogers either to provide a note or use brackets when supplying information from outside the resource itself. RDA makes an exception for such resources as naturally occurring objects that do not normally carry identifying information. In these cases, catalogers do not need to indicate that the information came from outside the resource itself:

```
245  00   $a Presentation easel.
500  ##   $a Title from distributor's catalog.
```

MARC Field 008

In MARC field 008, character positions 00 through 17 and 35 through 39 are defined the same way across all formats; this is where the date and place of publication and the language of the information resource are coded. Character positions 18 through 34 vary according to the type of record indicated in LDR/06. For cartographic materials, this is where the relief (008/18-21) and projection (008/22-23) are entered. For visual materials like projected media, the running time is entered in 008/18-20.

Sometimes the data elements do not make sense for a given type of record. For instance, two-dimensional graphic materials, kits, and realia are also visual materials with the same 008/18-20 as projected media, but those types of information resources generally do not have running times. In that case, the cataloger can consult the online *MARC 21 Format for Bibliographic Data* or OCLC's *Bibliographic Formats and Standards* and code "nnn" for not applicable.

FIGURE 3.2 | **Common record types for nonbook resources**

LDR/06	008/xx	Description (OCLC Mnemonic)	Sample Codes
e—Cartographic material	008/25	Type of cartographic material (CrTp)	a—Single map d—Globe e—Atlas
g—Projected medium	008/33	Type of visual material (TMat)	t—Transparency v—Videorecording
i—Nonmusical sound recording j—Musical sound recording	008/18-19	Form of composition (Comp)	nn—Not applicable pp—Popular music sg—Songs uu - Unknown
i—Nonmusical sound recording j—Musical sound recording	008/20	Format of music (FMus)	n—Not applicable
k—Two-dimensional nonprojectable graphic	008/33	Type of visual material (TMat)	i—Picture o—Flash card
m—Computer file	008/26	Type of computer file (File)	g—Game
o—Kit	008/33	Type of visual material (TMat)	b—Kit
r—Three-dimensional artifact or naturally occurring object	008/33	Type of visual material (TMat)	g—Game p—Microscope slide q—Model r—Realia w—Toy

Figure 3.2 shows record types of interest to nonbook catalogers, as well as the 008 byte that indicates some of the specific types of information resources that can be described. Only codes of particular interest to nonbook catalogers of juvenile material are listed, but other codes can be found in *MARC 21 Format for Bibliographic Data* and OCLC's *Bibliographic Formats and Standards*.

Note that for sound recordings, many of the 008/18-34 character positions are not applicable because they are more relevant to musical scores. For example, 008/33 indicates the transposition and arrangement of notated music.

MARC Field 006

As mentioned earlier, MARC field 006 is added to a bibliographic record to show additional information about the material being cataloged. It acts as an extension of MARC field 008 when an information resource has multiple format characteristics or when cataloging accompanying materials or kits. For example, the field is used to account for the computer file characteristics of electronic resources when the LDR/06 is not coded "m" for computer file.

MARC field 006 is needed to describe accompanying material only when the accompanying material is a different format than the primary resource. A student workbook and its answer guide are both texts, so MARC field 006 is unnecessary. A book with a read-along CD requires a MARC field 006 to account for the sound recording because the MARC field 008 only describes the text. Similarly, if a kit consists of different types of materials, they should all be accounted for in additional MARC 006 fields.

MARC Field 007

The physical description fixed field, or MARC field 007, contains coded information about the physical aspects of nonbook information resources. It is generally present when the following are nonbook materials: the primary resource being cataloged, any accompanying material, and any kit components. Because the MARC field 007 is repeatable like the MARC field 006, a bibliographic record may contain as many instances of the field as necessary.

As with MARC field 006, this fixed field is often filled out through a guided form in cataloging modules. After selecting the first byte—007/00, or category of material—the remaining data elements are defined accordingly. Figure 3.3 shows many of the MARC field 007 categories of material and corresponding

FIGURE 3.3 | **Selected MARC field 007 categories**

LDR/06 (Type of record) 006/00 (Form of material)	007/00 (Category of material)	007/01 (Specific material designation)
e—Cartographic material	a—Map	d—Atlas j—Map
	d—Globe	a—Celestial globe c—Terrestrial globe
g—Projected medium	g—Projected graphic	t—Transparency
	v—Videorecording	d—Videodisc f—Videocassette
i—Nonmusical sound recording j—Musical sound recording	s—Sound recording	d—Sound disc (audio CD) s—Sound cassette
k—Two-dimensional nonprojectable graphic	k—Nonprojected graphic	i—Picture k—Poster o—Flash card
m—Computer file	c—Electronic resource	b—Computer chip cartridge o—Optical disc (CD-ROM) r—Remote (Internet-based)
o—Kit	o—Kit	u—Unspecified

special material designations related to materials discussed in this chapter. Also included for reference are the corresponding LDR/06 (Type of record) and 006/00 (Form of material) codes.

Note that there is no MARC field 007 specifically intended for three-dimensional artifacts or naturally occurring objects. Some institutions code 007/00 as "z" for unspecified for these materials. Similarly, MARC field 007 is not often used to describe textual materials, although 007/00 can be coded "t" for text.

The 007/00 code for kits is included even though many catalogers choose instead to add MARC 007 fields that correspond to the different materials within the kit. For example, a curriculum set may include student texts, instructor texts, workbooks, posters, a CD-ROM, and a hand puppet. The LDR/06 is "o" for kit and the cataloger can enter MARC 006 and 007 fields for the poster (two-dimensional nonprojectable graphic) and the CD-ROM (electronic resource). A MARC 006 field can also be added for the hand puppet (three-dimensional object), but a MARC field 007 is not necessary.

MARC Fields 020 and 024

Unique identification numbers, such as ISBNs or UPCs (Universal Product Codes), should be included in the bibliographic record and can be used to identify and confirm usable copy cataloging records. Found on most books and sometimes on nonbook items, ISBNs are entered in MARC field 020, while the MARC 024 field is used for other standard identifiers, including the UPC, which is distinguished by first indicator "1." ASINs, or Amazon Standard Identification Numbers, and other unspecified standard numbers or codes may be entered in MARC field 024, with first indicator "8." Even though the ASIN will not be found directly on, or attached to, the information resource, it might be useful to include it in a bibliographic record because many libraries order materials through Amazon. Below are the UPC and ASIN for the Folkmanis Hen hand puppet:

024 #1 $a 638348030948.
024 #8 $a B01N9OCB74.

MARC Fields 245 and 246

The title and statement of responsibility for the information resource are recorded in MARC field 245. The title may be hard to determine on nonbook materials, appearing in different forms in different places. Sometimes labels on disc surfaces, containers, hang tags, or accompanying guides must be found and consulted.

Recorded in subfield $c, the statement of responsibility may be easy to determine, as on audiobooks with the same author as the print edition; or long, as on some videorecordings with multiple production companies; or hard to determine, as on a TI-84 graphing calculator, where some would enter Texas Instruments as the responsible party as well as the publisher in MARC field 264.

Variant titles are recorded in MARC field 246, sometimes with a note in subfield $i to indicate where the variant title is found. Below is an example of a video game with a couple of variant titles:

    245 00 $a PES2017 : $b pro evolution soccer.
    246 1# $i Title on accompanying booklet: $a PES 2017.
    246 3# $a Pro evolution soccer 2017.
    500 ## $a Title from container.

Record as many alternate or variant titles as necessary to ensure successful discovery.

Although it has since been superseded by MARC fields 336, 337, and 338 under RDA, the general material designation (GMD) in subfield $h of MARC field 245 can still be found in many AACR2-era (and later) bibliographic records. GMDs are assigned to some nonbook formats when cataloging according to AACR2, appearing immediately after the title proper in subfield $a and before the subtitle in subfield $b. This placement allows users to see quickly whether a title is in a special format, which is useful in catalogs where material type icons are not available. The list of GMDs is standardized, and the term appears in brackets in the record. Figure 3.4 shows selected GMDs that correspond to the types of materials that have been discussed in this chapter.

FIGURE 3.4 | **Selected GMDs for nonbook materials**

LDR/06 (Type of record)	General material designation (GMD)
e—Cartographic material	$h [cartographic material]
g—Projected medium	$h [transparency] $h [videorecording]
i—Nonmusical sound recording j—Musical sound recording	$h [sound recording]
k—Two-dimensional nonprojectable graphic	$h [flash card] $h [picture]
m—Computer file	$h [electronic resource]
o—Kit	$h [kit]
r—Three-dimensional artifact or naturally occurring object	$h [game] $h [microscope slide] $h [model] $h [realia] $h [toy]

Many institutions continue to use the GMD in their bibliographic records, even though MARC fields 336, 337, and 338 provide the same functionality. They prefer the GMD terms over the more technical ones found in the MARC 33x fields and will add the GMD to bibliographic records created under RDA that lack it. While other fields and codes are able to indicate the format and index the material in the catalog, the clarity provided by the GMD offers another means of targeting the desired resource in the catalog. Unfortunately, the authorized list of GMD terms is limited and will not be developed further as new kinds of material are added to library collections.

MARC Fields 260 and 264

When a bibliographic record is cataloged according to AACR2, the production, publication, distribution, or manufacture information is recorded in MARC field 260 without indicators. Under RDA, the same information is found in separate MARC 264 fields, with each function in a separate statement denoted by differing second indicators: production (0), publication (1), distribution (2), manufacture (3), and copyright date (4).

Some nonbook materials clearly display the place, name, and date of production, publication, distribution, and/or manufacture, but more often, these details are difficult to find. Many nonbook resources are not "published" in the same way that printed books are, and the information about a resource's issuance is often more correctly production or manufacture information, which should accurately be recorded in MARC field 264, second indicator "0" and "2," respectively. Detailed guidelines about when to select a specific function can be found in *MARC 21 Format for Bibliographic Data* and OCLC's *Bibliographic Formats and Standards.* However, in practice many catalogers still use MARC field 264, second indicator "1," for nonbook items that are not technically "published."

If the place and name of producer, publisher, distributor, or manufacturer cannot be determined, the bracketed phrases [place of producer not identified] and [name of publisher not identified] may be entered in their stead.

    260 ## $a Vernon Hills, IL : $b ETA/Cuisenaire, $c 2005.

    264 #1 $a Woodridge, IL : $b Wilton Industries, $c 2013.

    264 #2 $a Pawtucket, Rhode Island : $b Hasbro Gaming, $c [2012]

    264 #2 $a Wheeling, IL : $b Elenco Electronics, $c [2016]
    264 #4 $c ©2016

MARC Field 300

The physical description, including the extent and dimensions, of the nonbook resource and any accompanying material are recorded in MARC field 300. This field is repeatable, but in practice catalogers usually enter a single instance of this field and include more detailed physical description information in MARC field 500 notes. Accompanying material appears in subfield $e. Below are several examples of MARC 300 fields including, in order, a folded map, a DVD videodisc, an audio CD, a set of flash cards with a booklet in a box, a video game cartridge, an aptitude test (i.e., a kit), and a board game:

300 ## $a 1 map : $b color ; $c 61 x 85 cm, folded to 18 x 12 cm.

300 ## $a 1 videodisc (51 min.) : $b sound, color ; $c 4 3/4 in.

300 ## $a 1 audio disc (19 min.) : $b digital ; $c 4 3/4 in.

300 ## $a 22 flash cards : $b double sided, color ; $c 15 x 11 cm, in box 17 x 12 x 3 cm + $e 1 booklet (84 pages ; 16 cm)

300 ## $a 1 computer chip cartridge : $b sound, color ; $c 4 cm.

300 ## $a 1 Manual (vi, 59 pages ; 28 cm) ; 1 Fast guide (10 pages ; 22 cm) ; 25 identical Occupations index (22 pages ; 28 cm) ; 25 identical Assessment booklets (7 pages ; 28 cm) ; 1 pad score summary sheets ; $c in container 30 x 22 x 9 cm.

300 ## $a 1 game (1 game board, 45 cards, 12 pawns, 2 power-up tokens) : $b cardboard, plastic, color ; $c in box 27 x 27 x 5 cm + $e 1 instruction sheet.

Alternatively, for the last two examples—the kit and the board game—the cataloger could simply enter the following and include a MARC field 500 note to list the detailed contents of the kit and game, respectively:

300 ## $a 1 kit ; $c in container 30 x 22 x 9 cm.
500 ## $a Kit includes 1 Manual, 1 Fast guide, 25 identical Occupations index, 25 identical Assessment booklets, and 1 pad score summary sheets.

300 ## $a 1 game : $b cardboard, plastic, color ; $c in box 27 x 27 x 5 cm + $e 1 instruction sheet.
500 ## $a Game includes 1 game board, 45 cards, 12 pawns, and 2 power-up tokens.

MARC Fields 336, 337, and 338

The content, media, and carrier fields allow for increased specificity in describing the nature of the material described in the bibliographic record. MARC field 336 provides a more specific expression of content type than LDR/06 (Type of record), MARC field 337 can be used as an alternative or addition to the media type coded in 007/00 (Category of material), and MARC field 338 can be used as an alternative or addition to the carrier type coded in 007/01 (Specific material designation). The MARC 33x fields are repeatable, either to express multiple characteristics of a single resource or to describe different aspects of parts of the resource. Subfield $3 distinguishes which part of a kit or what accompanying material the field references.

Figure 3.5 is a table of content, media, and carrier types pertinent to the types of materials previously discussed in this chapter. For more terms and their codes—one-, two- and three-letter codes are in subfield $b—consult the *Term and Code List for RDA Content Types,* the *Term and Code List for RDA Media Types,* and the *Term and Code List for RDA Carrier Types.*

FIGURE 3.5 | **Common Content, Media, and Carrier types for nonbook materials**

336 (Content type)	337 (Media type)	338 (Carrier type)
cartographic image cartographic three-dimensional form	audio	audio cassette audio disc
computer program performed music sounds spoken word	computer	computer chip cartridge computer disc online resource
still image	microscopic	microscope slide
text	projected	overhead transparency
three-dimensional form two-dimensional moving image	unmediated	card object sheet volume
	video	videocassette videorecording

```
336  ##  $a cartographic three-dimensional form  $b crn  $2 rdacontent
337  ##  $a unmediated  $b n  $2 rdamedia
338  ##  $a object  $b nr  $2 rdacarrier
(a globe)
```

336 ## $a two-dimensional moving image $b tdi $2 rdacontent
337 ## $a video $b v $2 rdamedia
338 ## $a videodisc $b vd $2 rdacarrier
(a videorecording on DVD)

336 ## $a text $b txt $2 rdacontent
336 ## $a still image $b sti $2 rdacontent
336 ## $a spoken word $b spw $2 rdacontent $3 CD
337 ## $a unmediated $b n $2 rdamedia
337 ## $a audio $b s $2 rdamedia $3 CD
338 ## $a volume $b nc $2 rdacarrier
338 ## $a audio disc $b sd $2 rdacarrier $3 CD
{a picture book and accompanying read-along CD)

336 ## $a computer program $b cop $2 rdacontent
336 ## $a two-dimensional moving image $b tdi $2 rdacontent
337 ## $a computer $b c $2 rdamedia
338 ## $a computer chip cartridge $b cb $2 rdacarrier
(a video game on a computer cartridge)

MARC 5xx Fields

When cataloging nonbook materials, MARC 5xx notes fields are necessary to supply additional information to aid in identification, further describe contents, or explain accessibility requirements. Not every note field is relevant for every type of information resource. Consult the *MARC 21 Format for Bibliographic Data* and OCLC's *Bibliographic Formats and Standards* for detailed information about the different MARC 5xx fields and the data they contain. Under RDA, there is no prescribed order for MARC field 5xx notes, but many catalogers continue to list notes in the order dictated by AACR2.

MARC field 500 is the general note field for use when a more specialized note field is not applicable. It may be used to describe the colors or materials (plastic, felt, etc.) of a nonbook resource, the number of players for a game, bonus materials on DVDs, information about accompanying materials, unformatted contents, and many other things:

500 ## $a Title from hang tag.

500 ## $a Large, plush ladybug with red body and black spots, blue head, purple belly, and brown legs.

500 ## $a Kit includes: 3 rock specimens (granite, sandstone, and gneiss);
1 bag of rock and mineral fragments; 1 pair of tweezers; 1 magnet;
1 piece of glass; 1 piece of white porcelain; 1 magnifying glass; 2
mineral identification keys; 1 set of instructions.

Many of the specialized MARC 5xx notes are self-explanatory. MARC
field 505 (Formatted contents note) requires the use of specific punctuation
between elements and is often used to list separate tracks on sound recordings.
MARC fields 508 (Creation/production credits note) and 511 (Participant
or performer note) are particularly helpful in bibliographic records for sound
recordings, videorecordings, and even video games. However, catalogers do
not need to agonize over including every production company, musician, and
voice actor in their records.

The MARC 520 field (Summary, etc.) contains unformatted information
that describes the material, which usually explains the nature or purpose of
the resource rather than listing physical characteristics or quantities. If the
nonbook resource is considered appropriate for a specific audience or intellectual level, the information is recorded in MARC field 521 (Target audience
note). This may include reading grade level (first indicator "0"), interest age
(first indicator "1") or grade (first indicator "2"), and MPAA or ESRB rating
(first indicator "8"). MARC field 538 (System details note) contains technical
information about the resource—usually disc characteristics and equipment
requirements for videorecordings and computer resources:

505 0# $a Baby Beluga (2:39) -- Biscuits in the oven (2:24) -- Oats and
beans and barley (1:24) -- Day O (2:58) -- Thanks a lot (2:26) -- To
everyone in all the world (1:45) -- All I really need (3:44) -- Over in
the meadow (2:16) -- This old man (2:22) -- Water dance (1:52) --
Kumbaya (2:20) -- Joshua Giraffe (6:02) -- Morningtown ride (2:19).
508 ## $a Music composed by John Williams ; read-along produced by
Randy Thornton.
511 0# $a Read by Neil Patrick Harris.
520 ## $a Players campaign across the country, testing their knowledge
of United States presidents, history and geography. Features a U.S.
map game board, portraits of presidents, and over 900 questions.
521 8# $a ESRB Rating: E for everyone.
538 ## $a System requirements: PlayStation 4.

MARC Fields 100, 700, and 710

If it can be easily determined—for example, on audiobooks or musical sound recordings—a personal name may be recorded in MARC field 100 as the preferred access point, or main entry. However, for many nonbook materials, the title is the primary access point because no single person or body is responsible for the creation of the resource.

Whether or not MARC field 100 is present, any other individuals or bodies associated with the creation or production of the information resource should be entered in MARC fields 700 (Added entry—personal name) and 710 (Added entry—corporate name). Following RDA's guidelines, all these access points need to include $e for the relator term. Check the *MARC Code List for Relators* to find terms for everyone and everything connected to the information resource: composer, narrator, producer, voice actor, and more. Also consult the Library of Congress Authorities to make sure the correct forms of personal names and corporate bodies are being used.

> 100   1# $a Rowling, J. K., $e author.
>
> 700   1# $a Williams, John, $d 1932- $e composer.
>
> 700   1# $a Thornton, Randy, $e producer.
>
> 710   2# $a Melissa & Doug, $e manufacturer.

SUBJECT HEADINGS

In many ways, the descriptive cataloging rules of AACR2 and RDA are currently better equipped to handle nonbook materials than are subject cataloging schema. The *Library of Congress Subject Headings* (LCSH) and Sears headings generally describe what a resource is *about* rather than what it *is*. For example, the subject headings Video games and Hand puppets are for works about video games and hand puppets and not for the items themselves. LCSH and Sears headings are recorded in MARC field 650, second indicator "0" and "7," respectively. Sears subject headings also have subfield $2 with the term "sears" to indicate the source of the subject heading system.

However, LCSH can address the content as well as format of some nonbook materials. *The Library of Congress Subject Headings Manual* (SHM) has instruction sheets for applying subject headings to maps and atlases (H 1865), posters (H 1945.5), software (H 2070), and visual materials and non-music sound recordings (H 2230). There are form subdivisions to use with topical headings for maps ($v Maps), posters ($v Posters), software ($v Software and $v Computer games), and fiction films ($v Drama) about those topics.

When children are the intended audience for the resource, there are the form subdivisions $v Juvenile films, $v Juvenile software, and $v Juvenile sound recordings.

> 651   #0 $a United States $v Maps.
>
> 650   #0 $a World War, 1939-1945 $v Posters.
>
> 650   #0 $a Human anatomy $v Juvenile software.
>
> 650   #0 $a Penguins $v Drama.

LCSH cannot accommodate all types of nonbook materials, and many catalogers use the topical headings in MARC field 650 to express format anyway, for example, assigning Hens and Hand puppets to the Folkmanis Hen hand puppet mentioned earlier in this chapter, even though the resource is an actual hand puppet and not a treatise on chickens or puppetry. Another nontraditional application of subject headings is the use of both broader and narrower terms in a single bibliographic record. Usually catalogers are admonished to assign headings that are as specific as the topic covered in the resource, but children's catalogers, citing the different ways children search in catalogs, often assign a specific heading as well as a broader subject. Similarly, nonbook catalogers often use broader as well as specific terms. For the Folkmanis Hen hand puppet example, both Hens and Chickens can be assigned for improved discoverability.

GENRE AND FORM TERMS

If the local integrated library management system is set to index them, and if they are visible in the catalog, then genre/form terms in MARC field 655 can more properly be used to convey the format of nonbook materials. If the genre or form index term used in MARC field 655 comes from LCSH, then the second indicator is "0." If the term is from another source, the second indicator is "7" and the term is followed by subfield $2 with the code for the term's source, which can be found in the Genre/Form Code and Term Source Codes. Frequently used genre and form sources include the Library of Congress Genre/Form Terms ($2 lcgft) and the OLAC video game genre terms ($2 olacvggt).

> 655   #0 $a Planetariums.
>
> 655   #7 $a Manipulatives (Education) $2 lcgft
>
> 655   #7 $a Board games. $2 lcgft

655 #7 $a Children's maps. $2 lcgft

655 #7 $a Racing video games. $2 olacvggt

OLAC provides guidelines for the assignment of its video game genre terms, recommending using the term Video games as well as a more specific genre term. Likewise, in instruction sheet H 1913 for moving image genre/form terms, the SHM states that "headings may be assigned from different levels of the same hierarchy if desired," which seems to be common practice for nonbook materials, as discussed regarding subject headings earlier. After noting that the term "films" includes works released on video or digitally and "television programs" refers to works that were originally telecast, instruction sheet H 1913 provides detailed directions for assigning form and genre terms in MARC field 655, second indicator "7," and ending with subfield $2 lcgft.

Keeping in line with the types of materials so far discussed in this chapter, videorecordings should be assigned one of the following: Fiction films, Nonfiction films, Fiction television programs, or Nonfiction television programs. Depending on the running time of the film, Short films (for films less than 40 minutes) or Feature films (for films running more than 40 minutes) also need to be assigned. If the videorecording is produced with captions or sign language for the hearing impaired, add Films for the hearing impaired or Television programs for the hearing impaired. If the videorecording has additional audio description for the visually impaired, use Films for people with visual disabilities or Television programs for people with visual disabilities. If an individual library prefers, it can instead assign Video recordings for the hearing impaired or Video recordings for people with visual disabilities.

The best approach may be to use a combination of 650 subject headings and 655 form/genre terms, allowing for increased discoverability of nonbook materials.

650 #0 $a Kindness $v Juvenile films.
655 #7 $a Educational television programs. $2 lcgft
655 #7 $a Children's television programs. $2 lcgft
655 #7 $a Animated television programs. $2 lcgft
655 #7 $a Fiction television programs. $2 lcgft
655 #7 $a Television programs for the hearing impaired. $2 lcgft

For more information about subject analysis, including more application examples, see chapter 6.

CLASSIFICATION

Whether a library follows *Library of Congress Classification* (LCC) or Dewey, the classification number is based on the assigned subject headings. If a library decides to interfile its book and nonbook collections, this could lead to some interesting shelf-mates, as books about chickens will sit alongside hen hand puppets. It can also help students as they will find a model of the human brain next to books about the brain.

However, not all shelving systems can accommodate a variety of nonbook materials, so separating resources by format will probably be preferable. Non-fiction videorecordings may easily be classed using LCC or Dewey, and many public libraries opt to organize their fiction videorecordings by title. Decisions on shelving and classifying nonbook collections rely heavily on the available facilities and vary by library.

CONCLUSION

Part of being a good custodian of a library collection includes making all materials—book and nonbook—available to users in the catalog. It does not matter whether the circulating material requires a pair of reading glasses and a good light or a DVD player; it all belongs in the catalog. Happily, cataloging rules provide guidance for describing nonbook materials in bibliographic records, and subject headings and genre and form terms allow librarians to describe contents and formats using standardized language. All this enables users—children, students, teachers, and parents—to find what they are looking for, no matter the format.

RESOURCES

Art & Architecture Thesaurus Online. Getty Research Institute. Updated March 7, 2017. https://www.getty.edu/research/tools/vocabularies/aat/.

Intner, Sheila S. "Equality of Cataloging in the Age of AACR2," *American Libraries* 14, no. 2 (February 1983): 102-3. http://search.ebscohost.com/login.aspx?direct=true&db=a9h&AN=4952856&site=ehost-live&scope=site.

Library of Congress, Network Development and MARC Standards Office. *Genre/Form Code and Term Source Codes*. October 4, 2019. https://www.loc.gov/standards/sourcelist/genre-form.html.

———. *MARC 21 Format for Bibliographic Data.* 1999 edition, update no. 1 (October 2000) through update no. 28 (May 2019). www.loc.gov/marc/bibliographic/.

———. *MARC Code List for Relators.* May 9, 2016. www.loc.gov/marc/relators/.

———. *Term and Code List for RDA Carrier Types.* March 25, 2016. www.loc.gov/ standards/valuelist/rdacarrier.html.

———. *Term and Code List for RDA Content Types.* April 5, 2011. www.loc.gov/ standards/valuelist/rdacontent.html.

———. *Term and Code List for RDA Media Types.* April 5, 2011. www.loc.gov/ standards/valuelist/rdamedia.html.

Map Cataloger's Tool Box. www.acsu.buffalo.edu/~dbertuca/maps/cat/map-cat -toolbox.html.

Music Library Association. https://www.musiclibraryassoc.org/.

OCLC WorldCat Quality Management Division. *Bibliographic Formats and Standards,* 4th ed. www.oclc.org/bibformats/en.html.

OLAC Catalogers Network. https://www.olacinc.org/.

———. *Best Practices for Cataloging DVD-Video and Blu-ray Discs Using RDA and MARC2,* Version 1.1. November 2017. https://www.olacinc.org/sites/ default/files/DVD_Blu-ray-RDA-Guide-Version-1-1-final-aug2018-rev -1.pdf.

———. *Best Practices for Cataloging Video Games Using RDA and MARC21,* Version 1.1. April 2018. https://www.olacinc.org/sites/default/files/Video%20 Game%20Best%20Practices-April-2018%20Revision-a.pdf.

———. *Guidelines for OLAC Video Game Genre Terms.* October 2018. https:// www.olacinc.org/sites/default/files/Guidelines%20for%20OLAC%20 video%20game%20genre%20terms-revised.pdf. Olson, Nancy B., with the assistance of Robert L. Bothmann and Jessica J. Schomberg. *Cataloging of Audiovisual Materials and Other Special Materials: A Manual Based on AACR2 and MARC 21,* 5th ed. Westport, CT: Libraries Unlimited, 2008.

RDA Steering Committee. *RDA: Resource Description and Access.* American Library Association, Canadian Federation of Library Associations, and CILIP: Chartered Institute of Library and Information Professionals, 2010-.

———. RDA Toolkit. access.rdatoolkit.org.

4

CATALOGING CHILDREN'S MATERIALS USING RDA

MICHELE ZWIERSKI | Manager, Cataloging Services
Nassau Library System
Uniondale, New York

The library community has long recognized that children have their own unique characteristics and requirements as library users. Special bibliographic treatment of library materials is warranted to meet their needs. Many adult users of libraries—especially parents, teachers, school librarians, and other caregivers—also benefit from the special attention given to providing simple and full information about the content of library materials for younger readers.

When faced with creating a bibliographic record, a cataloger, especially one who is new to the task, can be overwhelmed. A cataloger should know how to search, edit, copy, create, and download records in a local online catalog. The content of the bibliographic record is created using international cataloging rules, with layers of rule interpretation and application. Content may also be created based on the needs of the local library community. This chapter will cover what to look for, how to describe, and how to transcribe information both recommended and required by current cataloging codes and practices. Don't become discouraged. Anyone who selects, purchases, recommends, and uses children's materials already has the knowledge necessary to build a solid bibliographic record.

The structure for a cataloging record is provided through use of the MARC format. The content choices and decisions for the record are created through application of the current cataloging code, RDA (Resource Description and Access).

RDA is the cataloging standard that replaced AACR2. RDA was introduced in 2010 but was not implemented until 2013. Even though RDA has been in use for more than a decade, catalogs still contain many records that were created by earlier standards (like AACR2 and previous standards). As a result, catalogs can be a mixture of old- and new-looking records. Today's cataloger needs to know what cataloging elements to embrace, what to ignore, and what needs to be updated.

RESOURCES

Even an experienced cataloger needs to look up rules and find examples during bibliographic record creation. Here are some basic resources.

RDA Toolkit (Referred to as RDA)

In order to use RDA Toolkit (online access to the cataloging rules), one must subscribe to it. Ordering information is available at https://www.rdatoolkit .org/subscribe. A print version is available for sale as well, providing a snapshot of the rules. The last print version is dated 2017.

MARC 21 Format for Bibliographic Data (Referred to as MARC 21)

Access is provided free through the Library of Congress (LC) at https://www .loc.gov/marc/bibliographic/. In addition to listing all the MARC tags, indicators, and subfields, this document is full of great examples created using RDA rules.

OCLC Bibliographic Formats and Standards (4th edition) (Referred to as OCLC BibFormat)

Access is provided free through OCLC at https://www.oclc.org/bibformats/ en.html. Although created for OCLC users, this document presents definitions and explanations for bibliographic record content. It is organized numerically by MARC field tags and gives many excellent examples of cataloging content. Also included is advice on basic cataloging concepts, such as "When to input a new record."

LOCAL CATALOGING POLICIES AND PROCEDURES

If these documents do not exist, then create them. Keeping track of cataloging decisions will not only be useful today, but in the future. Rules change, integrated library system (ILS) mechanics change, formats change, new library materials appear, old library materials disappear, and local librarians come and go. A cataloging policy and procedure manual will help local librarians maintain a calm approach to managing materials on shelves and in online catalogs.

When inputting an original cataloging record into an ILS, it can be overwhelming to try to use RDA Toolkit as a manual, checking rules to support any descriptive decisions made. It is helpful to take a moment to study the arrangement of RDA Toolkit.

The published version of RDA Toolkit is organized by a hierarchy that attempts to identify a resource not only physically, but also philosophically. This philosophical structure is known as WEMI:

Work: A distinct intellectual or artistic creation, that is, the intellectual or artistic content. For example, Beethoven's Ninth Symphony, when thought of in its essence, is a work.

Expression: An intellectual or artistic realization of a work in the form of alphanumeric, musical or choreographic notation, sound, image, object, movement, or any combination of such forms. For example, Beethoven's Ninth Symphony realized in musical notation is an expression.

Manifestation: A physical embodiment of an expression of a work. For example, a CD recording of a specific performance of Beethoven's Ninth Symphony is a manifestation.

Item: A single exemplar or instance of a manifestation. For example, a specific copy of a compact disc recording of the New York Philharmonic performing Beethoven's Ninth Symphony in 2018 is an item.

The bibliographic record in a library catalog is mostly the product of examining a Manifestation, or the physical embodiment of a work. The work and expression levels of a resource are used when creating authorized (i.e., structured) access points (e.g., titles and names). Keep these basic concepts in mind when using RDA Toolkit.

Before creating a new bibliographic record, search the local catalog. If an exact match is found, no new record needs to be created. See chapter 1 on copy cataloging for advice and instruction on matching and using existing records.

If there is not an exact match, there might be a near match that can be used as the foundation of a new record. For example, the material in hand is a spoken word edition of the book *A Heart in a Body in a World*. A cataloger would search the library's own catalog, then any available subscription bibliographic databases (e.g., OCLC, BookWhere, or SkyRiver) to see if there is an exact matching record (refer to chapter 1 for more detail). If no matching sound recording record is found for copy cataloging, the cataloger can "copy" the bibliographic record for the printed book. Most ILS systems have a Copy Record command available to catalogers. This copy of an existing record is now available for a cataloger to transform (or "derive") into a new record for the spoken word edition in hand. This new record would have to be edited to change the format from book to a spoken sound recording, adding the elements embodied by the sound recording version. Even though a "copy" is made of an existing record, this procedure is still considered to be new, or original, cataloging; previously, there was no bibliographic record for the spoken word version, but the cataloger has now created one.

If a cataloger cannot find any usable bibliographic record, a new record can be created from scratch. A new record template can be started inside the library catalog. This blank bibliographic record will include some basic MARC fields that can be filled in. If the library subscribes to a utility, a new record template can be activated in that product. Once the original cataloging record is completed and saved, the record can then be exported to a library's local catalog.

ORIGINAL CATALOGING WALK-THROUGH

Here is one suggested method to move through the creation of an original bibliographic record. Individual catalogers have their own dependable yet flexible procedures.

- Examine the resource (see below).
- Select the appropriate format (see below).
- Transcribe standard numbers (MARC tags: 020, 024).
- Transcribe the title page (MARC tags: 245, 250, and 264).
- Physically describe (MARC tag 300; RDA MARC tags 33x).
- Choose and add access points:
  » Determine creator (MARC tag 100).
  » Add contributors as access points (MARC tag: 7xx).
  » Add single or multiple series (MARC tag: 490 or 490/800;810;830).

- Add notes (MARC tag(s): 5xx as needed).
- Add subject access points (MARC tag(s): 6xx).
- Add classification (MARC tag 082/092 for Dewey or 050/090 for Library of Congress).

Examine the Resource

Always keep the user in mind. "If I wanted this exact thing, how would I look for it?" By orienting focus as a user, the cataloger can create a more useful cataloging record.

- For books, look at the title page, title page verso, cover, illustrations, bibliography, and index. Look for special features and accompanying material.
- For nonbook resources, examine the container and the contents.

After this preliminary inspection, a cataloging record can take shape.

Select the Appropriate Format: What Is This Thing?

In order to transcribe a record into an ILS, first determine the format. Is it a book? A video game? Is it a DVD with an accompanying CD, or a CD with an accompanying DVD? When entering a Format (or Type) MARC code into a template, the other default blank fields change to accommodate the unique characteristics of that format. A MARC bibliographic record for the book *Lord of the Flies* is different than the MARC record for the feature film version. The feature film cataloging record includes the technical aspects of that format as well as a list of the cast and crew. The MARC tags for these film elements may not show up in the template for an original book cataloging record.

If the format is not obvious, ask some basic questions. Is the resource meant to be read, listened to, or viewed? Where will this thing be shelved? The answers to these questions will guide a cataloger to the logical format.

OCLC BibFormat includes a list that gives common definitions for each format (with the MARC tags). The format section in this list is at https://www.oclc.org/bibformats/en/fixedfield/type.html.

Once the format decision is made, the cataloging template can be filled out.

CREATING A CATALOGING RECORD

In all examples, the variable fields begin with an implied $a. The definition of any MARC tag, along with valid indicator values and subfield codes, can be found in MARC 21. Additional advice and examples can be found in the MARC format appendix of this book.

The examples are meant to broadly illustrate what might be contained in these MARC fields. The examples are not comprehensive for the descriptive areas nor for the MARC tags and subfields.

Here are some of the most common fields used in children's cataloging.

Identifiers (RDA 2.15.1) (MARC 020, 024 and 028)

Enter numbers that are found on the resource. These could be standard numbers (like ISBN, UPC or Music Publisher numbers). For an ILS, sometimes standard numbers are used to capture and display cover art in the catalog.

ISBN (International Standard Book Number)
020 _ _ 9780972181938

UPC (Universal Product Code, or barcode)
024 1 _ 888295268196

Publisher or Distributor Number

Indicators define the type of number transcribed. In this example, the first indicator of 4 means a video recording publisher number. The second indicator instructs the ILS whether to generate a separate note for the online catalog.

028 4 2 DVD478 $b Weston Woods

Title Proper of Work (RDA 2.3) (MARC 245 $a with 246/740)

The title proper is a core element and required when cataloging using RDA. Locate the part of the resource that has the most information about the resource. For books, this is usually the title page. The title page and verso are often used as the source for much of the transcribed information. After the initial examination of a resource, a cataloger might find other titles (from the cover, from the spine, etc.) that can be entered into the bibliographic record in MARC fields 246 or 740. For nonbook material, examine the container as well for cataloging content.

Type in the title exactly as it appears. If an Arabic number is in the title, transcribe as a number. If the number is spelled out on the title page, spell it out in the 245 field.

245 1 4 The book with no pictures / $c B.J. Novak.

245 1 0 And Tango makes three / $c by Justin Richardson and Peter Parnell ; illustrated by Henry Cole.
246 3   And Tango makes 3

RDA has rules for typing conventions (capitalization, punctuation, and spacing). Many useful examples are found in MARC 21 and OCLC BibFormat.

Although not as common, RDA allows for the creation and usage of a Preferred title (MARC 130/240/730, also called Uniform title). This is a title or form of title that is chosen to identify a work, and is the form used as the authorized access point for that work. When a work appears in different versions, the Preferred title allows a chosen and structured way to search. The Preferred title is most commonly seen in cataloging records for translations and musical works.

<pre>
240 1 0 Divergent. $l Chinese
245 1 0 Fen qi zhe.
</pre>

By adding a Preferred title field to the cataloging record, all *Divergent* titles will sort and display together. Without the 240 field, it may not be clear that this book is a Chinese translation of *Divergent*.

<pre>
100 1 _ Beethoven, Ludwig, $d 1770-1827, $e composer.
240 1 0 Symphonies, $n no. 9, op. 125, $r D minor
245 1 4 The most famous symphony of all times [...].
</pre>

If a resource has a title that has no identifying elements, the 240 field will provide an authorized, consistent form of access.

Another use of a Preferred title is to differentiate between same-titled but completely different resources.

<pre>
130 0 _ Ghostbusters (Motion picture : 1984)

130 0 _ Ghostbusters (Motion picture : 2016)
</pre>

Statement of Responsibility (RDA 2.4) (MARC 245 $c)

After examining the resource and transcribing the title proper, continue to transcribe the rest of the information that may be available. This usually means transcribing any statements of responsibility that are associated with the resource.

The statement of responsibility is a statement relating to the identification and/or function of any agents responsible for the creation of, or contributing to the realization of, the intellectual or artistic content of a resource. As with the title, transcribe what is on the piece in the order found there.

<pre>
245 1 0 And Tango makes three / $c by Justin Richardson and Peter.
          Parnell ; illustrated by Henry Cole.
245 0 4 The house with a clock in its walls / $c Amblin Entertainment
          and Reliance Entertainment present ; a Mythology Entertainment
          production ; produced by Bradley J. Fischer, James Vanderbilt, Eric
          Kripke ; screenplay by Eric Kripke ; directed by Eli Roth.
</pre>

Edition Statement (RDA 2.5) (MARC 250)

An edition statement identifies the edition to which a resource belongs. Transcribe it exactly as it appears from any part of the resource. If the word "edition" is abbreviated on the piece, then it is transcribed as such.

> 250 __   Second edition.
>
> 250 __   Director's cut.
>
> 250 __   50th anniversary ed.

Sometimes a resource lacks an edition statement but proves to be different than other available editions. A cataloger can then create one that is descriptive of the changes. If the information created is obtained from a source outside the item in hand, bracket the information and add a note indicating the source.

> 250 __   [Deluxe edition].
>
> 500 __   Edition statement from record company's website.

Publication Statement (RDA 2.8) (MARC 264)

Place of publication, publisher's name, and date of publication are required for published materials.

A rule of thumb is to choose publication data that is prominent. Choose the most current date associated with the edition/version in hand. Again, transcribe as it appears on the source of cataloging information, such as the title page, or title page verso.

Publication statements on resources can be complicated. A title page might include multiple places of publication. The publisher's name might include the name of a subsidiary company or an imprint. There might be multiple dates, including copyright dates, dates of publication, printing dates, performance dates, and so forth. There might even be no publication information at all. Look for what is the most prominent (and reflective of what you have in hand) and transcribe as the publication statement. Although RDA does allow transcription of all publication data, a cataloger should consider transcribing only what is necessary for identification of an item.

> 264 _1   New York, NY : $b Simon & Schuster Audio, $c 2019.
>
> 264 _1   Milwaukee : $b [publisher not identified], $c 2020.

Extent (RDA 3.4) (MARC 3xx)

Extent includes both number of units (or pages) and dimension(s) (RDA 3.5). The field also includes a description of the content of the resource, such as illustrations (RDA 7.15).

> 300 _ _   450 pages : $b illustrations (some color) ; $c 23 cm.
>
> 300 _ _   1 online resource (1 audio file) : $b digital.
>
> 300 _ _   1 audio disc : $b digital ; $c 4 3/4 in. + $e 1 book (1 volume (unpaged) : color illustrations ; 23 x 32 cm).
>
> 300 _ _   1 volume (unpaged) : $b color illustrations ; $c 26 cm.

Many excellent examples can be found in OCLC BibFormat.

One major change from the previous set of cataloging rules (AACR2) and RDA is the addition of several 3xx fields to represent characteristics of the material being cataloged. These fields contain codes that can identify a resource as text, what type of musical score it is, or even if the sound is Dolby Digital. The most common of these new 3xx fields are 336, 337, and 338. The language for $a content is taken from RDA. A chart of these values with codes for $b and $2 is available at https://www.loc.gov/standards/valuelist/index.html.

Content Type (RDA 6.9) (MARC Tag 336)

Content type is the form of communication through which a work is expressed. Codes and values are charted at https://www.loc.gov/standards/valuelist/rdacontent.html.

For a printed book:
> 336 _ _   text $b txt $2 rdacontent

For a printed book with illustrations, add a second 336:
> 336 _ _   still image $b sti $2 rdacontent

For a DVD:
> 336 _ _   two-dimensional moving image $b tdi $2 rdacontent

Media Type (RDA 3.2) (MARC Tag 337)

Media type reflects the general type of intermediation device required to view, play, run, etc., the content of a resource.

Codes and values are charted at https://www.loc.gov/standards/valuelist/rdamedia.html.

For a printed book:

    337 __ unmediated $b n $2 rdamedia

For a CD-ROM:

    337 __ computer $b c $2 rdamedia

For a DVD:

    337 __ video $b v $2 rdamedia

Carrier Type (RDA 3.3) (MARC Tag 338)

Carrier type reflects the format of the storage medium and housing of a carrier in combination with the media type (which indicates the intermediation device required to view, play, run, etc., the content of a resource). Codes and values are charted at https://www.loc.gov/standards/valuelist/rdacarrier.html.

For a printed book:

    338 __ volume $b nc $2 rdacarrier

For a DVD:

    338 __ videodisc $b vd $2 rdacarrier

Creator (RDA 19.2) (MARC 100/110/111) (also known as Main Entry or Primary Access Point)

Contributors (RDA 20.1) (MARC 700/710/711) (also known as Added Entries)

A creator is person, family, or corporate body that is responsible for the creation of a work. The creator is a required element in an RDA cataloging record.

Often, there may be more than one author, a collaborating illustrator, or a lyricist involved in the creative process. RDA allows a cataloger to add all these contributors to the cataloging record, in notes (5xx) and as added access points (7xx). RDA also allows a cataloger to limit the number of access points.

If there is one creator (out of many) having principal responsibility, then this creator is required to be added as an access point (1xx). If more than one creator share responsibility, the first one named is added as an access point (1xx); add all others as additional access points (7xx).

For children's materials, LC practice is to provide an access point (7xx) for an illustrator. If there is more than one illustrator, LC recommends applying "cataloger judgement" to include an access point for more than the first listed.

Choosing the creator is sometimes tricky, given resources that have many collaborators (e.g., graphic novels and feature films). The choice of the 1xx field may also affect how materials are shelved. Many libraries traditionally add a line in call number spine labels for the creator or whatever name is listed in the 1xx field. For example, many libraries classify their fiction collection using the last name of the author as listed in the 100 field of the cataloging record.

A typical spine label might read FIC plus the first letters of an author's last name. Usually this is straightforward, but exceptions arise. For example,

> All keyed up / $c Matt Christopher ; text by Stephanie Peters ; illustrated by Daniel Vasconcellos.

The author Matt Christopher died in 1997, but many books continue to be published with his name appearing prominently. These new books, when cataloged, will not have Matt Christopher as the 100 entry. The new author of the new book should be the 100. A librarian has to decide whether the spine labels of the new books read FIC Christopher (not matching the 100 field, but keeping all Matt Christopher books together on the shelf) or scatter the new books so that the spine labels match the new author (in this example, FIC Peters for Stephanie Peters).

The form of the name used in access points in bibliographic records will be the "authorized" form. The authorized form of a heading is recorded in authority records. The most widely used authority file is the one maintained by LC (https://authorities.loc.gov/). Read chapter 5 for further advice.

RDA allows for the addition of a "relationship designator" or "relator term" to name access points (personal and corporate names: 100, 110 and 700, 710). This term indicates the nature of the relationship between entities represented by the authorized access points. In the example below, the "relationship" B. J. Novak has with this resource is one of authorship.

For the creator having principal responsibility:

> 100 1 _   Novak, B. J., $d 1979- $e author.

For other associated creators, use the 7xx fields. An example would be resources with two authors and an illustrator:

> 100 1 _   Richardson, Justin, $d 1963- $e author.
> 245 1 0   And Tango makes three / $c by Justin Richardson and Peter Parnell ; illustrated by Henry Cole.
>
> ....
>
> 700 1 _   Parnell, Peter, $e author.
> 700 1 _   Cole, Henry, $d 1955- $e illustrator.

When cataloging a resource that includes multiple creators and collaborators, RDA allows a cataloger to decide how many more access points to include beyond the required first named creator and first named illustrator (for children's materials). If the local decision is made to limit the number of 7xx fields to include in bibliographic records, then a decision needs to be made about which creators and/or collaborators to choose. For example, if a user is searching for a feature film, then names that would be logical to search are director, writer, and important actors. Take the reasonable expectations of a library user into account when establishing cataloging policies and procedures.

In an online catalog with keyword searching, almost every word becomes an access point. But with keyword searching, the results are often voluminous and murky. With an access point that is structured and authorized, search results become quicker and more valuable. Searching the heading Richardson, Justin in a Name Index dialog box of an online catalog will give more successful appropriate results than searching Justin Richardson in a keyword dialog box.

Series Statements (RDA 2.12) (MARC Tag 490 and 800/810/830)

Materials for children are often published in one or more series. A series is a group of related materials. In nonfiction materials, the series might reflect the publisher, an author or a subject theme.

> Kingfisher knowledge.

> Kingdom classification.

In fiction materials, a series might involve a character or a connected story line.

> Nate the Great.

> I survived!

Materials in series are extremely popular. If the user enjoys one book in a series, there is comfort and excitement in finding the next in the series. Both adults and children fall enthusiastically into reading series. Therefore, being able to easily discover these series on the shelf and in a library's catalog is extremely important.

The first step is to transcribe the title as it appears on the resource into the MARC tag 490. If the series has numbering associated with it, add the number of the series in the $v of the 490 field.

> 490 1 _   Diary of a wimpy kid ; $v 3

> 490 1 _   Book 1 of The Cade saga

> 490 1 _   39 pistas

The associated MARC tag 800/810 or 830 will hold the "authorized" form of the series title. The authorized form is a version of a heading that has been constructed with the RDA rules in mind. See chapter 5 for more information and advice.

By adding an access point (in this case, an 800/810 or 830) in the authorized form for each title in a series, a cataloger guarantees a consistent method of searching, retrieving, and displaying that particular series.

> 800　1_　Kinney, Jeff. $t Diary of a wimpy kid ; $v 3.
>
> 800　1_　Stewart, Paul, $d 1955- $t Edge chronicles. $p Cade saga ; $v 1.
>
> 830　_0　39 clues. $l Spanish.

Note Area (MARC Tags 5xx)

The Note Area is a place where a cataloger has an opportunity to describe the material in hand, in addition to transcribing bibliographic information from the resource.

In RDA, there are instructions for adding notes to cataloging records. These instructions are scattered throughout RDA. For instruction on specific types of notes, use RDA Toolkit's search box to move to corresponding rules.

Here are some examples of common notes, including important notes for children's materials. For a complete list of 5xx fields, with definitions (including indicators and subfields) and examples, see the MARC 21 documentation at https://www.loc.gov/marc/bibliographic/bd5xx.html.

500　General Note

Use for information not covered by more specific notes. Both indicators are blank.

> 500　__　Includes index.
>
> 500　__　Issued on Playaway Launchpad, a pre-loaded learning tablet.
>
> 500　__　In the title the word "Amazing" is lined through.

504   Bibliography, etc.

Use to indicate presence of a bibliography, discography, filmography, webography, etc.

> 504 _ _   Includes bibliographical references (page 54).
>
> 504 _ _   Includes bibliographical references (pages 33-35) and index.
>
> 504 _ _   "List of songs sung by Pete Seeger": pages 56-58.

505   Contents Notes

This field contains titles of separate works, titles of parts of an item, or a table of contents. Capitalization and punctuation are prescribed. Through use of the indicators, the contents note can be labelled as incomplete or partial, when appropriate.

There are two different encoding styles of a 505 field: basic and enhanced. In the basic version (second indicator of blank), the entire contents note is entered in $a. In the enhanced version (second indicator of zero), different elements of the note are separately tagged (with repeatable subfields) to allow more detailed retrieval and indexing.

Examples of both kinds are available in MARC 21 site or in the OCLC BibFormat at https://www.oclc.org/bibformats/en/5xx/505.html.

> 505   0 _   What is a Labradoodle? -- The Labradoodle look -- Puppy time -- Caring for Labradoodles -- Darling doodles.
>
> 505   0 0 $t What is a Labradoodle? -- $t The Labradoodle look -- $t Puppy time -- $t Caring for Labradoodles -- $t Darling doodles.
>
> 505   0 _   Kleine Nachtmusik, K. 525. Romance / Mozart (National Arts Centre Orchestra, Mario Bernardi, conductor) (5:38) -- Méditation / Contant (Moshe Hammer, violin ; Tsuyoshi Tsutsumi, violoncello ; William Tritt, piano) (3:17) -- Sonata in C minor. Andantine expressivo / Pescetti (Judy Loman, harp) (4:17)
>
> 505   0 0 $t Kleine Nachtmusik, K. 525. $t Romance / $r Mozart (National Arts Centre Orchestra, Mario Bernardi, conductor) $g (5:38) -- $t Méditation / $r Contant (Moshe Hammer, violin ; Tsuyoshi Tsutsumi, violoncello ; William Tritt, piano) $g (3:17) -- $t Sonata in C minor. $t Andantine expressivo / $r Pescetti (Judy Loman, harp) $g (4:17)

520 Summary, etc. Note

This could be a summary, abstract, annotation, review, or any other phrase describing the material. The first indicator will generate a display constant. A display constant is machine-generated data that will automatically display on the public screen based on the indicator values chosen for a MARC field. For example, a first indicator of blank will generate "Summary" at the start of a note field. A first indicator of 3 in the 520 field will generate "Abstract" at the start of the note field.

For children's materials, the 520 field presents an opportunity for a cataloger to add details that may not fit into any other part of the bibliographic record. Words that are in the 520 are available for keyword searching in most ILS systems and may enhance access.

The Library of Congress Children's and Young Adults' Cataloging Program (CYAC) gives guidelines for creating concise, consistent summaries. Some general advice:

- Follow the University of Chicago's *Manual of Style*.
- Use present tense and active voice.
- Mention the name and age of the main character, where appropriate, as well as the setting, time period, and key elements of plot or theme.
- Try not to give away too much of the story, particularly the ending.
- Keep the summary note twenty-five to thirty words in length.

See the CYAC website at https://www.loc.gov/aba/cyac/summaries.html for fuller instructions.

521 Target Audience Note

This information identifies the specific audience or intellectual level for which the content of the described item is considered appropriate. The first indicator will display a label identifying the content. A first indicator of "8" supplies no display constant.

The form of the content is not specified by RDA. When there are no instructions given, generally, a cataloger transcribes the form that is used on the material. These notes can help parents and educators quickly understand the age, reading, or interest level of the material.

> 521 1 _ 009-012.
> (the interest level for this material is ages 9 through 12)

> 521 1 _ Ages 9-12.

> 521 2 _ K-1.
> (the interest level for this material is grades Kindergarten through 1)

521 8 _   MPAA rating: PG-13.

521 8 _   Guided reading level: P.

586 *Awards Note*

Information on awards associated with the item in hand. Indicators will generate a display constant. For example, a first indicator of 8 displays no label.

586 _ _   Printz Award, 2019

586 _ _   Academy Award, Best Picture, 1961

Subject Access Points (MARC Tag(s): 6xx)

Subject analysis is outside the scope of RDA. See chapter 6 on subject analysis.

Classification (MARC Tag 082/092 or 050/090)

Classification is outside the scope of RDA. See chapter 8 on Dewey Classification.

CONCLUSION

Keeping a catalog consistent is the best public service that librarians can provide for their community. On-site and remote users benefit from a catalog that produces reliable information easily. Library staff also benefit from a clean catalog when ordering and processing library materials.

Getting It Right

A new or inexperienced cataloger might be overly cautious when creating and editing catalog records. Material (especially new material) that sits in the cataloger's office loses value within the library collection. Material should start circulating as soon as possible. Strike a balance between creating perfect records and records that might be perfect enough. Concentrate on transcribing information accurately and adding notes and access points that are important to the community. A cataloger can always return to records to correct and update. All catalogers make mistakes. All catalogers acknowledge, correct, and move on.

Local Editing Practice

It may be tempting to enhance a catalog by adding unique local (and perhaps nonstandard) data to bibliographic records. Making local cataloging choices may seem like the only way to help the community find and use the collection. Use caution in adding this type of information to the local catalog. Cataloging records that are purchased from vendors or downloaded from utilities will not have those local edits so, any cataloging record from an outside source will have to be changed manually to add any local edits. Catalog searches will quickly become less comprehensive and soon become unreliable.

For example, let's say that a teacher wants to be able to search and retrieve all the books on their second grade reading list. As the librarian, you agree to do this by adding a local note "2nd grade reading list" (as MARC tag 590) to the bibliographic record.

The first thing to check is whether the MARC tag chosen to add to a record is searchable in the ILS (both in cataloging and in public modes). If a record with the local information is not found when searching by that local information, then there is no point to adding it to the record.

The library may own multiple versions/editions of a title. If it is one of the books on the teacher's list, which bibliographic record needs the note added? The book? The book with CD? The DVD? The e-book? Will one record be selected to include the local note? Will the local note be added to all the records? Without the local note being on all records for all versions of this title, there is no guarantee that this title will be found.

What happens when the teacher adds titles or deletes titles from the list? What happens to the catalog when that teacher moves or retires? Someone will have to maintain and update these edited records so that the catalog is current and correct. It is not an impossible service to offer to this teacher, but the process is not as simple as it appears.

Practice

Learn about cataloging by looking at many catalog records. Look at the cataloging records already used in the catalog. Take the material in hand and look at the choices that were made to create that record. Remember, though, that catalogs contain a wide variety of records, created using different cataloging codes and policies. Consistency among records may not be reality. At the very least, comparing one record with material in hand can provide some insight into bibliographic record creation.

If there is another library catalog that performs well, contact the librarian or cataloger behind it. Having another experienced librarian/cataloger available for advice is invaluable. Remember always that a cataloger provides a very public service to all library users. Keep the user in mind and heart when creating thoughtful, accurate bibliographic records.

ADDITIONAL RESOURCES

There are several sources for "best practices" and additional help and advice when cataloging children's materials in all formats.

The Children and Young Adults' Cataloging Program at the Library of Congress (https://www.loc.gov/aba/cyac/index.html) is responsible for creating cataloging data for most children's fiction. The website includes Library of Congress practice for addressing issues specific to children's materials.

The OLAC (On-Line Audiovisual Catalogers) website, (https://www .olacinc.org/), is an excellent source for information and advice on all things nonprint. Subscribe to its electronic discussion list, OLAC-L.

The American Library Association's Association for Library Collections and Technical Services (ALA-ALCTS) maintains a website, Resources for Catalogers of Children's Materials, (www.ala.org/alcts/resources/org/cat/ childrens).

Electronic discussion lists, such as Listservs, can be a great place to post questions. LC maintains a list of library discussion lists at https://www.loc .gov/rr/program/bib/libsci/guides.html#listservs. This list includes information for subscribing to AUTOCAT (for all things cataloging and classification) and LM_NET (for school library media specialists).

LOOKING AT AUTHORITY RECORDS

PATRICIA RATKOVICH | Catalog Librarian
University of Alabama

The primary focus of this chapter is to present the reader with a brief overview of the authority control process, including examples of how to interpret and apply authority records. This chapter presents the basic concepts, ideas, and examples of the most common types of authorized headings that one might encounter. This will provide the librarian with the knowledge necessary for performing authority control tasks, as well as the motivation to do independent reading and investigation of this topic.

Librarians should be familiar with at least some concepts about authority work. According to a survey of library science faculty, the following concepts support a framework for an essential working knowledge of what a new librarian needs to know about authority work (Taylor 2004, 47):

- what authority control is
- why authority control is important
- why authority control is important to users in information retrieval
- how authority control is accomplished

WHAT IS AUTHORITY CONTROL?

Authority control provides a standardized access point for forms of names, titles, and subjects with cross references from different forms that may be in use. Authority control is the recording of a standardized access point to make the catalog searchable under one heading. All records with related or associated names, subjects, and additional access points are retrieved in the catalog with one search.

WHY IS AUTHORITY CONTROL IMPORTANT? WHY IS IT IMPORTANT IN INFORMATION RETRIEVAL?

These two questions go hand in hand. Even though catalogs offer more specific searches, such as author, subject, or title, keyword searching is the most common form of searching for both children and adults. Searching by keyword brings up many irrelevant hits, which can cause real frustration. If a person is known by different names, or the series title appears differently on different books, the user would have to search separately under all those different forms in order to find every catalog entry for that person or series title. Computers read only what is in the record. They cannot tell if a name, title, or series is spelled correctly and cannot recognize any variants that might relate to an authorized heading. An authority record can bring many forms of a heading together under one authorized form. This allows for cross references to point the user to the authorized heading. These "see" and "see also" cross references are helpful aids that alert the user to identical and similar topics, respectively.

HOW IS AUTHORITY CONTROL ACCOMPLISHED?

An authority record with the authorized form of the heading and any related forms is added to the library's online catalog. This is an informational record, coded in the MARC authority format, that points users to the authorized version of a heading. Once at the authorized heading, a user can comprehensively see all resources that relate to that name, title, or subject. Usually, when the bibliographic record is saved or brought into the catalog, the authority control process compares the access points in the bibliographic record against the authority files. This identifies any need for a change in the bibliographic record. Authority records are not static. They evolve and change and require updating as terminology, status, language, and definitions change in society.

The most common way of accomplishing authority control is by using records established in authority files, such as those of the Library of Congress. Local authority records can be created and maintained in-house. These would reflect any local decisions made, for example, classification decisions for a series or special directions for cataloging an item that requires the use of that authority record. Authority records created by others can also be used (provided they are willing to share the records). Any local information added to an authority record must be updated and maintained by the librarian. If any local 4xx or 5xx fields are added to an authority record, those records must be tracked and maintained by the librarian. If the authority record is updated from an external source, the local updates may be lost. The most commonly used files of authority records are those from the Library of Congress Name Authority File (LCNAF) and *Library of Congress Subject Headings* (LCSH). There is an abundance of these records, each of which can be downloaded to the local catalog free of charge. There are other subject heading lists one can use, including the *Sears List of Subject Headings,* and the *Art & Architecture Thesaurus,* but these are not free. The Library of Congress updates existing authorities and creates new authorities as needed. Vendors can help a library manage the authority work and can provide a wide range of authority services designed for various budgets.

Authorized headings and authority records are also developed specifically for use in cataloging material for children and young adults. LC's Children's and Young Adults' Cataloging Program (CYAC) develops children's headings for use in bibliographic records and provides cataloging for material published for children and young adults in the United States (see https://www.loc.gov/aba/cyac/). They also create the authority records for the LCNAF. These terms are helpful in bibliographic records that children will be searching. Another list of headings to consider is the *Sears List of Subject Headings,* developed with small and medium libraries in mind, where it is still widely used.

MAchine Readable Catalog (MARC) formats are used for both bibliographic records and authority records. Some tags (three-digit field numbers) may seem to be the same but are defined differently for use in a bibliographic record or authority record. Here are some examples of authority records from the LCNAF (online), formatted according to *MARC 21 Format for Authority Data.*

Personal Names

When seeking a name authority for a person known as Pink, one might think that not many people really use that as a name. However, a search for an authority record for this name results in two possibilities:

```
LC control no.: n 2006209683
LCCN Permalink https://lccn.loc.gov/n2006209683
HEADING: Pink, 1974-
000   00512nz a2200169n 450
001   6923389
005   20060803020112.0
008   060713n| acannaabn |a aaa
```

```
010  __   $a n 2006209683
040  __   $a DLC $b eng $c DLC
100  0_   $a Pink, $d 1974-
400  1_   $a Laksana, I Ketut, $d 1974-
400  1_   $a Ketut Laksana, I, $d 1974-
400  0_   $a I Ketut Laksana, $d 1974-
667  __   $a Not same as Laksana, I Ketut Darma (n 91088675)
670  __   $a Butterflies of Bali, 2005: $b t.p. (Pink) p. 14 (I Ketut . Laksana; b.
          1974)
953  __   $a wj15
```

and

LC control no.: no2001005090

LCCN Permalink: https://lccn.loc.gov/no2001005090

HEADING: P!nk, 1979-

```
000  01107cz a2200253n 450
001  5281946
005  20141223073823.0
008  010122n| azannaabn |a aaa c
010  __   $a no2001005090
035  __   $a (OCoLC)oca05397583
040  __   $a PPi-MA $b eng $e rda $c PPi-MA $d IAhCCS $dPPi-MA
          $d IAhCCS $d IEN
046  __   $f 19790908
100  0_   $a P!nk, $d 1979-
370  __   $a Abington (Pa.) $c United States $2 naf
374  __   $a Singers $a Composers $a Actresses $2 lcsh
375  __   $a female
400  0_   $w nne $a Pink, $d 1979-
400  1_   $a Moore, Alecia, $d 1979-
510  2_   $w r $i Corporate body: $a You+Me (Musical group)
670  __   $a Pink. Most girls [SR] p2000: $b label (Pink)
670  __   $a http://www.pinknews.f2s.com, Jan. 19, 2001 $b (Pink; real
          name, Alecia Moore; b. Sept. 8, 1979)
670  __   $a Now that's what I call music. 31, p2009: $b container (P!nk)
670  __   $a All-music guide, July 20, 2009 $b (Pink (professionally known as
          P!nk!))
670  __   $a Wikipedia, May 16, 2013 $b (Pink; stylized as P!nk; born Alecia
          Beth Moore, September 8, 1979, Abington Township, Montgomery
          County, Pa.; American singer-songwriter, musician, and actress)
```

These two authority records present similar types of information for each person, using the standard MARC fields for authority records. A full authority record (Maxwell 2002, 37) contains the following elements:

1. The heading (1xx field).
2. A citation for the item being cataloged that generated the need for the heading (first 670 field) and additional citations as necessary (additional 670 fields).
3. Cross-references if needed and appropriate (4xx and 5xx fields).
4. Other fields as necessary.
5. Certain fixed field values.

The 1xx field contains the authorized heading for the name. Comparing the two records, note that each has a "d" subfield, which contains a birth date that allows a person to distinguish it from any other person named Pink. Also, in order to distinguish which Pink is the creator of the material being cataloged, the 374 (occupation) field or 670 (note) holds additional information that might clarify any distinction. When cataloging materials created by Pink, the musician, one would use the heading Pink, 1979- in the bibliographic record. If the materials were created by P!nk, the butterfly-book contributor, use Pink, 1974- in the bibliographic heading.

If a book gives the author's name in any particular form, as for the books by Lemony Snicket, that is the name under which to search for the authority record. The authority record gives the occupation (field 374) as author. The 375 field indicates that his gender is male. The 400 fields give different forms of his name that have been used in other languages. The 500 field gives his identity as Daniel Handler. Finally, the 678 field (biographical or historical data) tells us that Lemony Snicket is a pseudonym. This is a valid, authorized name, so it can be used.

The full authority record for the author who is known as Lemony Snicket is:

```
LC control no.: n 99020360
LCCN Permalink:https://lccn.loc.gov/n99020360
HEADING:Snicket, Lemony
000   01157cz a2200301n 450
001   3716841
005   20120901074923.0
008   990312n| azannaabn |b aaa
010   __   $a n 99020360
035   __   $a (OCoLC)oca04942029
040   __   $a DLC $b eng $e rda $c DLC $d DLC $d OCoLC $d UPB
046   __   $f 19700228
```

053	_0	$a PS3558.A4636
100	1_	$a Snicket, Lemony
374	_	$a Author $2 lcsh
375	_	$a Males $2 lcgdt
377	_	$a eng
400	1_	$a Сникет, Лемони
400	1_	$a למוני, סניקס
400	1_	$a1, סניקס, למוני. ברא, תיריא. טסיוקלה _$w r $i Real identity: $a
500	1_	$w r $i Real identity: $a Handler, Daniel
667	_	$a Machine-derived non-Latin script reference project
667	_	$a Non-Latin script references not evaluated
670	_	$a The bad beginning, 1999: $b CIP t.p. (Lemony Snicket)
670	_	$a Phone call to pub., 03/12/99 $b (Lemony Snicket also uses the name: Daniel Handler)
670	_	$a Wikipedia, 28 August 2012 $b (Lemony Snicket is the pen name of American novelist Daniel Handler (born February 28, 1970))
678	0_	$a Lemony Snicket is a pseudonym of American author Daniel Handler (1970-)
953	_	$a lb13 $b lh06

A search for an authority record for actress Elizabeth Taylor leads to the dilemma of different persons with similar names. More than eighteen authority records are returned. In each case, the record for a given resource is entered under the name used on the item itself. Knowing that the Elizabeth Taylor being searched for was an actress and died after 2010 helps narrow the search to two possibilities:

LC control no.: n 50009560
LCCN Permalink: https://lccn.loc.gov/n50009560
HEADING: Taylor, Elizabeth, 1932-2011

000	01701cz a2200397n 450
001	3262387
005	20181004073302.0
008	800331n| azannaabn |a aaa

010	_	$a n 50009560
035	_	$a (OCoLC)oca00045078
040	_	$a DLC $b eng $e rda $c DLC $d DLC $d Uk $d DLC $d UPB $d InU $d UPB
046	_	$f 1932-02-27 $g 2011-03-23 $2 edtf
100	1_	$a Taylor, Elizabeth, $d 1932-2011
368	_	$c Americans $2 lcdgt

370 __ $a Hampstead (London, England) $b Los Angeles (Calif.) $2 naf

374 __ $a Actors $2 lcdgt

374 __ $a Actor $2 itoamc

375 __ $a Females $2 lcdgt

377 __ $a eng

400 1_ $a Hilton, Elizabeth, $d 1932-2011

400 1_ $a Wilding, Elizabeth, $d 1932-2011

400 1_ $a Todd, Elizabeth, $d 1932-2011

400 1_ $a Fisher, Elizabeth, $d 1932-2011

400 1_ $a Burton, Elizabeth, $d 1932-2011

400 1_ $a Jenkins, Elizabeth, $d 1932-2011

400 1_ $a Taylor, Elizabeth Rosemond, $d 1932-2011

400 1_ $a Taylor, Liz, $d 1932-2011

400 1_ $a Warner, Elizabeth, $d 1932-2011

670 __ $a Nibbles and me ... 1946

670 __ $a Elizabeth Taylor, the last star, c1981: $b t.p. (Elizabeth Taylor) CIP galley (married John Warner 12/4/76; Liz)

670 __ $a Elizabeth Taylor, 2000: $b p. 310 (became Dame Commander of the Order of the British Empire, Spring 2000)

670 __ $a msnbc.msn online, Mar. 23, 2011 $b (Elizabeth Taylor; d. Wed [Mar. 23, 2011], Los Angeles, age 79)

670 __ $a Wikipedia, Mar. 23, 2011 $b (Elizabeth Rosemond Taylor; b. Feb. 27, 1932, Hampstead, district of North London; d. Mar. 23, 2011; also known as Liz Taylor; English-American actress)

678 0_ $a Elizabeth Taylor (1932-2011) was an English American actress.

952 __ $a RETRO

953 __ $a xx00 $b td03

and

LC control no.: n 91118171

LCCN Permalink: https://lccn.loc.gov/n91118171

HEADING: Taylor, Elisabeth D.

000 00881cz a2200193n 450

001 2146961

005 20120315152604.0

008 911120n| acannaabn |a aaa

010 __ $a n 91118171 $z n 86110524

035 __ $a (DLC)n 91118171

040 __ $a DLC $c DLC $d DLC

100 1_ $a Taylor, Elisabeth D

```
400  1_  $a Taylor, Liz
400  1_  $a Taylor, Elizabeth, $d 1931-2012
500  1_  $a McNeill, Elisabeth
670   _  $a Curtis, T. 20th century antiques, c1989: $b t.p. (Elisabeth D.
             Taylor) jkt. (hist., U. of Aberdeen; freelance journalist; has pub.
             novels under pseud Elisabeth McNeill)
670   _  $a Her Cash in on collecting, c1986: $b t.p. verso (Liz Taylor)
670   _  $a Scotsman WWW site, Mar. 15, 2012 $b (Elizabeth Taylor; b. 25
             Apr. 1931, Fife; d. 6 Mar. 2012, Melrose; journalist; wrote historical
             novels under the name Elisabeth McNeill; univ. education at
             Aberdeen)
953   _  $a ea14 $b bf11
```

Because the dates for birth and death are close, they are not very helpful. The first names are spelled differently, an important detail found by reading the records closely. The first authority record has a 374 field that contains the word "actor," so it must be the right one. Look at the 400 fields. Elizabeth Taylor had several name changes throughout her career. These are "see from" references, which direct the cataloger away from the searched name, as this is a non-authorized heading. The 100 field contains the authorized form of the name. For example, if a catalog search were made for Hilton, Elizabeth, the user would be redirected to Taylor, Elizabeth, 1932-2011. It is important to read authority records carefully, as they are meant to help the cataloger determine which form of the name to use in the cataloging record being created for each resource. In the second authority record (for Elisabeth D. Taylor), there is another valid heading (identified by a 500 field tag). The instruction is to use the form Taylor, Elisabeth D. when it appears that way on the resource. However, use the authorized heading McNeill, Elisabeth for historical novels written by this same person, who has two distinct bibliographic identities.

An even better-known example of an author writing under more than one name is Dr. Seuss (Seuss, Dr., 1904-1991). His authority record lists three other authorized names, each of which contains the same birth and death years: Geisel, Theodor Seuss; LeSieg, Theo; and Stone, Rosetta. When an author has published under different names (e.g., Lemony Snicket or Dr. Seuss), the cataloging of each resource is entered under the name used in the resource itself.

Series Title

One of the most important functions of authority work is to bring together like items. If children have enjoyed the first book in the series, they will often want to read the next one. The authorized series title is a way to help users and librarians find multiple titles in a series. Two of the most common types of series authority records used are the name/title series and preferred (uniform) title series. Here is an example of a name/title series authority record:

LC control no.:n 99020366
LCCN Permalink: https://lccn.loc.gov/n99020366
HEADING:Snicket, Lemony. Series of unfortunate events
000   00714cz a2200241n 450
001   3251367
005   20150524122626.0
008   990312n| azabaaaan |a aaa
010   __ $a n 99020366
035   __ $a (OCoLC)oca04942036
040   __ $a DLC $b eng $e rda $c DLC $d DLC $d ICrIF
100   1_ $a Snicket, Lemony. $t Series of unfortunate events
370   __ $g New York (N.Y.)
373   __ $a HarperCollins (Firm)
380   __ $a Series
430   _0 $a Series of unfortunate events
642   __ $a bk. 1 $5 DPCC $5 DLC
643   __ $a New York $b HarperCollins
644   __ $a f $5 DLC
645   __ $a t $5 DPCC $5 DLC
646   __ $a s $5 DLC
670   __ $a The bad beginning, 1999: $b CIP t.p. (A series of unfortunate
              events, book the first)
953   __ $a lb13 $b lb14

The user would not need to know individual titles of the books, but only the author or series title. The individual bibliographic records for each title would have a 490 field with the form of series title as it appears on the resource, and an 8xx as the authorized heading, which may differ. An 800 field in a bibliographic record consists of the personal name of the author and the title of the series. Here is an abbreviated example of a bibliographic record with a series traced differently:

100   1_ $a Snicket, Lemony
245   1 4 $a The bad beginning / $c by Lemony Snicket ; illustrations by
              Brett Helquist

....

490   1_ $a A series of unfortunate events ; $v book 1
800   1_ $a Snicket, Lemony. $t Series of unfortunate events ; $v book 1

Looking back at the series authority record for *A Series of Unfortunate Events* above, the 100 field in the authority record gives the form of that name and the title to use. Other things can be learned from the authority record. The 400 and 430 fields both contain "see from" tracings. If one were to look up one of the "see from" headings in the catalog, one would then refer back to the authorized heading in the 100 field. Then the 642 field gives an example of the enumeration format that should be used in the bibliographic record (i.e., whether there is a part or volume designation as well as the number in the series).

The 644, 645, and 646 fields contain information important to the library's treatment of the series.

1. The 644 field tells the librarian which analysis decisions were made about the series. The listed subfield codes indicate that all (f—analyzed in full), some (p—analyzed in part), or none (n—not analyzed) of the volumes in the series are analyzed.
2. The 645 field indicates whether the series is indexed (t—traced as a series) or not (n—not traced as a series).
3. The 646 field indicates whether the series is classed as a collection (c—collection), classed separately (s—separately), or if it is a subseries classed with another series (m—classed with main series). If classed together (c), each individual bibliographic record for each title in the series share the same base call number. If classed separately (s), all the call numbers are different. If the series is a subseries, it is classed with another series or the main series.

An authority record for a preferred (uniform) title contains the same fields as those found in a name/title series record, but instead of a 100 field in the authority record there is a 130 for the preferred title. In the bibliographic record for series, titles include a 490 field, transcribing the way the series appears on the book, and a 730 or 830 field containing the preferred title.

```
LC control no.: no2013007294
LCCN Permalink: https://lccn.loc.gov/no2013007294
HEADING: Little Prince (Graphic Universe (Firm))
000   00912cz a2200241n 450
001   9179871
005   20140306073916.0
008   130121n| azaaaaaan |a ana c
010   __   $a no2013007294
035   __   $a (OCoLC)oca09388179
040   __   $a IOrQBI $b eng $e rda $c IOrQBI $d IWhI $d IOrQBI
```

```
046  __  $k 2012
130  _0  $a Little Prince (Graphic Universe (Firm))
380  __  $a Series (Publications) $a Monographic series $2 lcsh
400  1_  $w nne $a Dorison, Guillaume. $t Little Prince
400  1_  $a Bruneau, Clotilde. $t Little Prince
642  __  $a bk. 1 $5 DPCC
643  __  $a Minneapolis, MN $b Graphic Universe
644  __  $a f $5 IOrQBI
645  __  $a t $5 DPCC $5 IOrQBI
646  __  $a s $5 IOrQBI
670  __  $a Dorison, Guillaume. The Planet of Wind, c2012: $b t.p. (The Little
          Prince) cover (The Little Prince; book 1)
670  __  $a Bruneau, Clotilde. The planet of the Overhearers, 2013: $b t.p.
          (The Little Prince) cover (The Little Prince ; book 7)
```

Note that the bibliographic record for this particular title would include a 490 field transcribing the series title from the resource, and a 830 field giving the preferred title for this series:

```
490  1_  $a The Little Prince ; $v bk. 1
830  0_  $a Little Prince (Graphic Universe (Firm)) ; $v bk. 1
```

Subject

People use language to communicate with one another, but adults normally modify their speech when they talk to children, using different words to communicate an idea or concept to a juvenile in order to facilitate their understanding. It is the same in the catalog. When cataloging any material that children are going to be accessing in the library catalog, there are things to keep in mind, no matter which subject heading source is used. Using the *Library of Congress Children's Subject Headings* in the bibliographic record allows young users to search on familiar terms and common language terms that they already know. Children are learning vocabulary terms constantly in school, at home, and in public. They use language differently from the way that adults do. When cataloging material that is intended to be used by children and young adults, catalogers must remember this. Here are examples of subject authority records for a type of spider:

```
LC control no.: sj 96005581
LCCN Permalink: https://lccn.loc.gov/sj96005581
HEADING: Funnel-web spiders
000  00411cz a2200169n 450
```

```
001   4878549
005   20120404094725.0
008   960509|| anbnnbabn |a ana
010  __   $a sj 96005581
035  __   $a (DLC)sj 96005581
035  __   $a (DLC)225234
040  __   $a DLC  $c DLC
150  __   $a Funnel-web spiders
450  __   $a Agelenidae
906  __   $t 9699  $u te05  $v 0
952  __   $a ANNOTATED CARD PROGRAM SUBJECT HEADING
953  __   $a xx00
```

and

```
LC control no.: sh 85002168
LCCN Permalink: https://lccn.loc.gov/sh85002168
HEADING: gelenidae
000   00602cz a2200241n 450
001   4655431
005   20120320084108.0
008   860211i| anannbabn |b ana
010  __   $a sh 85002168
035  __   $a (DLC)sh 85002168
035  __   $a (DLC)2116
040  __   $a DLC  $c DLC  $d DLC
053  _0   $a QL458.42.A3
150  __   $a Agelenidae
450  __   $a Agalenidae
450  __   $a Funnel weavers
450  __   $a Funnel-web spiders
450  __   $a Grass spiders
550  __   $w g  $a Spiders
670  __   $a Syn. liv. org.:  $b v. 2, p. 89
670  __   $a Kaestner invert. zoo.:  $b v. 2, p. 190
906  __   $t 8536  $u fk03  $v 0
953  __   $a ff0
```

The Library of Congress uses the 010 field (LC control number) as a unique identifier for each authority record. The letters "sj" before the number identify the subject heading as juvenile (CSH) versus the letters "sh" (subject heading), which is LCSH. Funnel-web spiders (above) is the authorized form of the subject when using the LC children's subject headings list, versus the Agelenidae (scientific name) used in LCSH subject headings. Each has a 450 field that contains a "see from" reference tracing pointing to the other term.

Geographic Names

Geographic names found in the 151 field of authority records are used as 651 subjects in bibliographic records. A person interested in spiders may only want information about spiders in North Carolina, or even more specifically, on spiders in Newton Grove, North Carolina. Geographic locations allow the cataloger to pinpoint a region, state, city, or town in which a story or event takes place.

Looking at the authority record for Las Vegas, New Mexico, it is seen that the authorized geographic heading is in the 151 field. This geographic heading was established using the sources cited in the 670 fields. The 781 field contains the form of this heading if it is to be used as the geographic subdivision under a subject heading. If a young user were searching the topic "industrialization" and the record had a geographic subdivision, she or he could narrow the topic to the name of a city or town. For example, a record with the subject entry 650 _0 $a Industrialization $z New Mexico $z Las Vegas is used for a resource about industrialization in the New Mexico town of Las Vegas. On the other hand, a general resource about the town would simply contain the geographic heading: 651 _0 $a Las Vegas (N.M.).

```
LC control no.: n 81133683
LCCN Permalink: https://lccn.loc.gov/n81133683
HEADING: Las Vegas (N.M.)
000   00992cz a2200217n 450
001   3789716
005   20100513071631.0
008   820108n| acannaabn |a ana
010 _ $a n 81133683
034 _ $d W1051326 $e W1051326 $f N0353538 $g N0353538 $2
      geonames
035 _ $a (OCoLC)oca00678548
040 _ $a DLC $b eng $c DLC $d NmU $d WaU $d OCoLC
043 _ $a n-us-nm
151 _ $a Las Vegas (N.M.)
451 _ $w nnaa $a Las Vegas, N.M.
451 _ $a New Town (Las Vegas, N.M.)
```

670 __ $a Perrigo, Lynn Irwin. Papers, 1968-1980: $b (until 1882 referred
        to as New Town; 1882-1884 incorporated as City of Las Vegas
        (along with Old Town); 1884-1903 disincorporated, administered by
        County Commission; 1903-1970, City of Las Vegas (separate from
        City of East Las Vegas); 1970- City of Las Vegas (combined with
        previously separate City of East Las Vegas))
670 __ $a GeoNames, algorithmically matched, 2009 $b (ppl; 35°35′38″N
        105°13′26″W)
781 _0 $z New Mexico $z Las Vegas
952 __ $a RETRO
953 __ $a xx00

This chapter describes the most common types of authority records, with explanations of coded information in authority records. It is important to always read through the complete authority record carefully to determine whether the person or concept described in the authority record matches the person or concept of the resource in hand. Correctly input the authorized heading into the bibliographic record.

Other types of authority records not discussed in this chapter are genre headings (655 field), corporate headings (110/610/710) and conference headings (111/611/711 fields). These types of headings are included in the Library of Congress authority file. For examples of format and coding in all fields, refer to *MARC 21 Format for Bibliographic Data*.

It is essential for any library catalog to use standard authorized headings for names, preferred (uniform) titles, and subject terms. For names and preferred titles, U.S. libraries should use Library of Congress authorized headings (see https://authorities.loc.gov/). Subject headings may either be used from the *Sears List*, *Library of Congress Subject Headings*, or *Library of Congress Children's Subject Headings*, but should not be mixed in the same record. Often, however, cataloging records from vendors or downloaded from online sources use more than one type of heading in order to accommodate a variety of local policies. In such cases, the local library's cataloging staff should always make the corrections necessary for compatibility with the subject authority used locally. If possible, the local online catalog should have software for loading authority records into the online catalog. This way, errors and discrepancies in bibliographic record headings can be caught and corrected automatically.

Because there are several types of headings that can be considered "names" or "subjects," such as form and genre terms, it will be helpful to refer also to chapter 6, "Subject Headings for Children's Materials," for further explanation about various types of headings.

Consistency is paramount. Users must be able to find all resources in the catalog by or about one person, work, or organization under a single form of entry. Similarly, subject headings must be consistent, so that users doing a subject search will find all available resources on that single subject. Understanding and using authority records will help in this discovery challenge.

RESOURCES

Library of Congress, Network Development and MARC Standards Office. "What is a MARC Record, and Why Is It Important? Parts I -VII." In *Understanding MARC Authority Records: Machine Readable Cataloging* (January–July 2019): https://www.loc.gov/marc/uma/pt1-7.html.

Maxwell, Robert L. *Maxwell's Guide to Authority Work.* Chicago: American Library Association, 2002.

Taylor, Arlene G. "Teaching Authority Control." In *Authority Control in Organizing and Accessing Information: Definition and International Experience*, edited by Arlene G. Taylor, Barbara B. Tillett, Mauro Guerrini, and Murtha Baca, 43-57. Binghamton, NY: Haworth Information Press, 2004.

6

SUBJECT HEADINGS FOR CHILDREN'S MATERIALS

MICHELE ZWIERSKI | Manager, Cataloging Services
Nassau Library System
Uniondale, New York

The process of cataloging a resource for a library collection can be separated into three parts: descriptive cataloging, subject analysis, and classification. This chapter will provide an overview of the subject analysis process and a brief overview of commonly used subject lists and thesauri.

During the descriptive cataloging process, a cataloger will examine the material and transcribe information provided on the piece. By the completion of this phase, the cataloger has a pretty good idea of what the resource is about and where it will best be shelved within the library collection. This "idea" can then be transformed into subject headings, which will point to a classification number.

In a cataloging record, subject concepts are translated into subject headings by using an authorized vocabulary list or thesaurus (controlled vocabulary). By using an agreed-upon form of entry from a chosen thesauri, a cataloger can build a consistent subject heading index for an online catalog.

The most commonly used subject heading list in library catalogs comes from the Library of Congress (LC). The *Library of Congress List of Subject Headings* (LCSH) is available for free use (and free download) at https://www.loc.gov/aba/publications/FreeLCSH/. As well, LC maintains and provides subject authority records (also free; individual records from the LC Authority file can be viewed and downloaded at https://authorities.loc.gov/). An online catalog holds bibliographic records and authority records, both in the MARC format. The authority records provide pointers (or references) to and from related access points. (See chapter 5 on authority work for more information.)

In addition to the LCSH, LC also maintains a separate subject thesaurus for use with children's materials. The *Children's Subject Headings* (CSH) list is maintained by the Children's and Young Adults' Cataloging Division (CYAC). New CSH headings are created when LCSH does not provide age-appropriate terminology. For example, LCSH uses the term "Delphinidae," whereas CSH uses the term "Dolphins." Instructions for access and use of the CSH list are available at https://www.loc.gov/aba/cyac/childsubjhead.html.

LCSH allows the use of subdivisions to further delineate a concept. For children's materials, for example, the subdivisions Juvenile fiction or Juvenile literature can be added to any LCSH term to separate the materials for adults from the materials for children. In a catalog for a collection that holds both children's and adult materials, having resources for children clearly labelled in the bibliographic record and, therefore, in displayed search results is important.

When subject headings are used from a specific list, MARC coding will reveal the source thesaurus. The second indicator points to a thesaurus. When needed, a further subdivision of $2 can be used to specify other alternate authorized thesauri.

- LCSH with a form subdivision

    650 _0 Dogs $v Juvenile literature.

- CSH (identified by the second indicator)

    650 _1 Dogs.

GENRE HEADINGS

Subject headings are used to describe what library materials are about. Genre terms are used to describe what the library materials *are*.

    655 _7 Clay animation films. $2 lcgft

    655 _7 Historical fiction. $2 lcgft

LC has been including genre headings in catalog records since the 1980s. Beginning in 2007, LC began to create authority records for genre terms. Authority records not only document the established form of a heading, but also include instructions for use. Here is an excerpted example of an authority record for a genre heading:

010 _ _ gf2014026330.
155 _ _ Fan fiction.
455 _ _ Fanfic.
670 _ _ Oxford English dict. online, Apr. 4, 2006 $b (fan fiction: fiction, usually fantasy or science fiction, written by a fan rather than a professional author, esp. that based on already-existing characters from a television series, book, film, etc.; (also) a piece of such writing; also fanfic or fan fic).
670 _ _ Internet fictions, 2009: $b p. 44 (Fan fiction--non-profitable, non-commercial texts based on other fictional texts (series, movies, and books) and written by their fans--has boomed with the development of the internet, to which it has moved from privately printed fanzines) p. 46 (initially, fans' activities were based in Usenet and then Yahoo message groups; then they were largely relocated to the forums, and nowadays towards blogs; fan fiction's set of internal genres includes «missing scenes» fanfiction, «Alternative Universe» fan fiction (AU) where the whole canon may be completely changed, and «crossovers» combining different sources in one story).
680 _ _ $i Fiction that incorporates characters and/or settings of books, television programs, etc., of which the authors are fans.

Since 2007, LC has continued to maintain these various authority files and has worked with subject expert communities to develop genre terms for specific types of resources (e.g., film and music). For more information visit the LC page at https://www.loc.gov/librarians/controlled-vocabularies/.

BISAC Headings

The book industry maintains the Book Industry and Standards Communication list (BISAC), which is used in bookstore categorization. Because of the browsable nature and consumer familiarity with commercial bookstores, some libraries have not only reconfigured their collections to match BISAC shelving arrangement but also added BISAC terminology to online catalogs.

LCSH

650 _0 Dogs $v Juvenile literature.

BISAC

650 _7 Pets / Dogs / General $2 bisacsh.

FAST Headings

Faceted Application of Subject Terminology (FAST) are subject headings that are derived from LCSH. FAST was developed in an attempt to simplify subject heading creation in a faceted, easy, and more modern way.

650 _7 Dogs. $2 fast

650 _7 Juvenile works. $2 fast

Sears Headings

See chapter 7 on the *Sears List of Subject Headings,* which is widely used in school library catalogs.

During the subject analysis phase of the cataloging process, a cataloger has a wide array of established thesauri from which to choose. Many of the bibliographic records available from LC or commercial vendors come with more than one set of subject headings. For example, the book *Game Changer* by Tom Greenwald can be cataloged to include all these subject headings:

650 _0 Football stories.
650 _1 Football $v Fiction.
650 _0 Sports injuries $v Juvenile fiction.
650 _0 Coma $v Juvenile fiction.
650 _0 Hazing $v Juvenile fiction.
650 _0 Dysfunctional families $v Juvenile fiction.
650 _1 Family problems $v Fiction.
650 _7 JUVENILE FICTION $x Health & Daily Living $x Diseases, Illnesses
         & Injuries. $2 bisacsh
650 _7 JUVENILE FICTION $x Social Themes $x Peer Pressure. $2
         bisacsh
650 _7 JUVENILE FICTION $x Sports & Recreation $x Football. $2 bisacsh
650 _7 Epistolary novel. $2 lcgft
650 _7 Fiction. $2 fast
650 _7 Juvenile works. $2 fast

One can see that, although all headings contribute to a richer discovery experience, it may become unwieldly to commit to adding all headings to all records. Copy cataloging records from bibliographic utilities or from vendors may include valid subject headings from more than one list. Evaluate which subject headings are best for the community and use the controlled vocabulary list(s) that include those headings. Discuss and document the cataloging decisions made. A cataloging unit should maintain consistency and efficiency when processing resources for collections.

Before setting policy, investigate how subject headings are indexed in the local library catalog. Some integrated library systems (ILSs) may be set up to include in the subject index only the 6xxs that have a second indicator of zero (LCSH) and not index any of the other subject headings. Other ILS settings might not include all content of all 6xx fields in the keyword index. Be sure to confirm what is searchable in what index before setting policy and procedures.

If a library catalog uses multiple subject sources, there is the risk of conflicting headings. For example, if LCSH and CSH headings are left in (or added to) catalog records, search results might conflict or separate in a displayed index. For example, in a catalog that accepts records with subject headings (with associated subject authority records) from multiple thesauri, a search for children's dystopian stories might result in split indexes.

If a catalog were to include LCSH headings only, a user could see clearly which dystopian books were for children and which ones were for adults.

> 650 _ 0   Dystopias $v Juvenile fiction. (valid LCSH heading for a children's fiction book about dystopia).

> 650 _ 0   Dystopias $v Fiction. (valid LCSH heading for an adult fiction book about dystopia).

If this catalog also included CSH headings, the intended audience distinction would suddenly become lost.

> 650 _ 0   Dystopias $v Juvenile fiction. (valid LCSH heading for a children's fiction book about dystopia).

> 650 _ 0   Dystopias $v Fiction. (valid LCSH heading for an adult fiction book about dystopia).

> 650 _ 1   Dystopias $v Fiction. (valid CSH heading for a children's fiction book about dystopia).

In the above index, a user browsing the subject access heading, Dystopias $v Fiction, would need to examine the records more closely before choosing. It would not be immediately clear if the book was intended for adults or children.

If this catalog also included genre headings, the index might appear as:

> 650 _ 0   Dystopias $v Juvenile fiction.
> (valid LCSH heading for a children's fiction book about dystopia).

> 650 _ 0   Dystopias $v Fiction. (valid LCSH heading for an adult fiction book about dystopia).

650   _1   Dystopias $v Fiction. (valid CSH heading for a children's fiction book about dystopia).

655   _7   Dystopian fiction. $2 gsafd (valid LC genre heading for any fiction book about dystopia).

In the above example, only the first subject heading clearly identifies children's books.

When setting a subject analysis policy for a catalog, one option would be not to include CSH headings in the catalog, resulting in:

650   _0   Dystopias $v Juvenile fiction. (valid LCSH heading for a children's fiction book about dystopia).

650   _0   Dystopias $v Fiction. (valid LCSH heading for an adult fiction book about dystopia).

655   _7   Dystopian fiction. $2 gsafd (valid LC genre heading for any fiction book about dystopia).

Or, a cataloger building a catalog for children's materials might create a policy to use only CSH and genre headings, resulting in:

650   _1   Dystopias $v Fiction. (valid CSH heading for a children's fiction book about dystopia).

655   _7   Dystopian fiction. $2 gsafd (valid LC genre heading for any fiction book about dystopia).

Whatever policy is created, remember to keep the end user in mind. Catalog users usually do not know the intricacies of subject thesauri and subject analysis application. Test any policies by searching results in the OPAC. Become the user.

CONCLUSION

Subject headings are an opportunity for a librarian to add consistent conceptual content and format content to a cataloging record that may not have been included elsewhere in the record. This content is then searchable, either by a subject search or in a general keyword search.

RESOURCES

Fountain, Joanna F., "Using LC's Children's Subject Headings in Catalogs for Children and "Young Adults: Why and How." In *Cataloging Correctly for Kids*. 5th ed., edited by Sheila S. Intner, Joanna F. Fountain, and Jean Weihs, 115-28. Chicago: ALA Editions, 2011.

Library of Congress. *Children's Subject Heading List.* www.loc.gov/aba/cyac/childsubjhead.html.

———. *Introduction to Children's Subject Headings*. PDF available at https://www.loc.gov/aba/publications/FreeLCSH/freelcsh.html#CSH.

———. *Introduction to Library of Congress Genre/Form Terms for Library and Archival Materials*, 2019 edition. PDF available at https://www.loc.gov/aba/publications/FreeLCGFT/freelcgft.html#Introduction.

7

THE SEARS LIST OF SUBJECT HEADINGS

MICHELE ZWIERSKI | Manager, Cataloging Services
Nassau Library System
Uniondale, New York

Subject analysis allows a cataloger to enrich the record with terms that might not be included in the descriptive portion of a bibliographic record. Subject lists and thesauri provide guidance and specific vocabulary when building this part of the bibliographic record.

In 1897, the Library of Congress began to establish subject headings for use in its catalog. By the time *Subject Headings Used in the Dictionary Catalogues of the Library of Congress* was published in 1909, the American Library Association had already released its own *List of Subject Headings for Use in Dictionary Catalogs.*

Both lists were based on the catalogs of large libraries. The ALA list found its origins in the Boston Athenaeum, Peabody Institute, and the *Harvard Subject Index.*

A successful subject heading list will describe concepts in the language of its users. As these new subject lists were being applied to collection descriptions in the early part of the twentieth century, local user groups saw a need for improvement. Even today, in the twenty-first century, new subject lists and thesauri are being developed by groups to better serve their communities.

The cataloging needs of small libraries, including school and public libraries, are different from the cataloging needs of the large libraries that began using the Library of Congress or the ALA subject lists in the early 1900s. Minnie Earl Sears (1873-1933) began to imagine an alternative subject heading list that would function better in smaller libraries. She examined the catalogs of several small libraries and began to put together her own list.

In 1923, Sears joined the publishing house of H. W. Wilson and produced the *List of Headings for Small Libraries* (later renamed the *Sears List of Subject Headings*).

The *Sears List* is unique among subject heading lists in that it does not attempt to be a complete list of terms used in any single library. Rather, it is a list of only the headings most likely to be needed in a typical small library that serves as a skeleton or pattern for creating other headings as needed. By using the *Sears List* as a foundation, the cataloger in a small library can develop a local authority list or file that is consistent in form and comprehensive for that library. This has proven over the years to be a practical and economical solution to the cataloging needs of small libraries, including school and public libraries.

The 22nd edition (2018) is the most current print edition of the *Sears List*. In 2018, Grey House Publishers acquired the *Sears List* from H. W. Wilson. For the most up-to-date information, Grey House Publishers offers the *Sears List* as an online subscription database (https://searslistofsubjectheadings .com/). A Spanish translation of the *Sears List of Subject Headings* (*Sears: Lista de encabezamientos*, 2008) is also available from Grey House Publishing.

One of the strongest features of the list is its choice of common terms for subject concepts:

Library of Congress Subject Heading	Sears List heading
Swine	Pigs
Illegal aliens	Unauthorized immigrants
Agkistrodon piscivorus	Cottonmouth
Older people	Elderly

It is important to remember when using the *Sears List* that not every single subject heading is listed in the resource. For example, the subject Rats is not listed in the *Sears List* but can be added as a valid Sears subject heading to any appropriate bibliographic record. This topical subject heading is created in accordance with the guidelines set up in *Principles of the Sears List of Subject Headings* (available in the print version or for free download at https:// searslistofsubjectheadings.com/page/principles) This great resource provides an overview of the *Sears List*, including principles of subject analysis and the mechanics of constructing Sears subject headings.

One of the efficiencies of the cataloging process is copy cataloging. This involves finding matching bibliographic records for owned materials and then "copying" this record into an online catalog. Sears subject headings are beginning to appear more frequently in the widely shared Library of Congress MARC bibliographic records. Because of this, Sears headings are becoming more commonplace in cataloging records. By using a record that already contains Sears headings, a cataloger can accept the subject analysis decisions made, rather than having to assign Sears headings locally to every record.

Another cataloging efficiency may be to contract a library services firm (e.g., MARCIVE or Backstage Library Works) to examine any current and future MARC records in a catalog for correction and enrichment, including the addition of Sears subject headings. Publishers, when providing MARC records, may also include Sears subject headings.

As cautioned in other chapters of this book, the subject heading index of an online catalog can easily (and quickly) become flooded with competing and conflicting terms. There are many lists and thesauri of subject headings available for use in library catalogs. If the catalog holds a "dominant" set of subject headings (e.g., from the *Library of Congress Subject Headings* or from *Sears*), one should carefully assess the impact of adding any new additional sets of headings. For example, if a catalog uses Sears headings, materials about Pigs would have the subject heading of Pigs. If the *Library of Congress Subject Headings* (LCSH) were suddenly allowed entry into this catalog, there would be conflict when searching by subject:

Pigs (valid Sears subject heading)

and

Pigs *see* **Swine** (from the valid LCSH)
Swine (valid LCSH)

and

Swine *see* **Pigs** (from the valid Sears subject heading)

Maintaining consistency in an online catalog is a critical part of a cataloger's mission. The online catalog is the entryway for remote users to discover and request resources. Carefully consider the impact a new subject vocabulary will have on the existing cataloging records before making any changes.

In conclusion, the *Sears List* is a well-established, beloved subject heading list used by libraries, both small and large. Using popular terms for subject concepts allows users of all ages, especially children, to remotely explore online catalogs successfully. By allowing catalogers to create structured new headings as needed, the *Sears List* easily provides agility and currency.

RESOURCES

American Library Association. *List of Subject Headings for Use in Dictionary Catalogs.* Boston: Library Bureau, 1895.

Bristow, Barbara A., ed. *Sears List of Subject Headings.* Ipswich, MA: H. W. Wilson/Grey House Publishing, 2018.

Calimano, Iván E. and García, Ageo. eds. *Sears: Lista de Encabezamientos de Materia: Nueva Traducción y Adaptación de la Lista Sears.* New York: H. W. Wilson, 2008.

Library of Congress. *Subject Headings Used in the Dictionary Catalogues of the Library of Congress.* Washington, DC.: Library of Congress, 1909.

Miller, Joseph. "Sears List of Subject Headings." In *Cataloging Correctly for Kids*, 5th ed., edited by Sheila S. Intner, Joanna F. Fountain, and Jean Weihs, 129-34. Chicago: American Library Association, 2011.

Principles of the Sears List of Subject Headings. Grey House Publishing, 2018.

A free resource that explains general principles of subject analysis and specifically how the List is applied is at https://searslistofsubjectheadings.com/page/principles.

DEWEY DECIMAL CLASSIFICATION

ALEX KYRIOS
OCLC, Inc.

The Dewey Decimal Classification (DDC) is the world's most widely used library classification system. It is particularly used extensively in public libraries and school libraries in the United States. Its numbers are widely recognizable as part of shelfmarks, most commonly known as call numbers, on spine labels. Its strengths also shine through in digital systems, which process numbers more easily than natural language. This chapter provides an overview of how to use the DDC at a local library.

DDC FORMATS

The DDC is published online via WebDewey, a proprietary system maintained and licensed by OCLC. Traditionally, the DDC was published in print volumes on a seven-year cycle, with each full edition followed by an abridged edition. Abridged editions were published in single volumes. The last traditional print Dewey products were Edition 23 (2011) and Abridged 15 (2012); full editions consisted of four volumes each from Edition 20 (1989) onward. Because the complexity of the full DDC was often unnecessary, the abridged edition was frequently used in cataloging for children, especially in school libraries.

With WebDewey making continuous updates to the classification, OCLC no longer publishes new print editions (including abridged editions) on a seven-year cycle. Catalogers may still use abridged classification when applying the DDC. Catalogers preferring a print format or having unreliable internet access can order a print-on-demand (POD) version of the full classification. Rather than being issued as separate editions, POD versions come from data that is pulled annually from WebDewey.

CHOOSING NUMBERS

The DDC is organized first by ten *main classes*:

000	Computer science, information & general works
100	Philosophy & psychology
200	Religion
300	Social sciences
400	Language
500	Science
600	Technology
700	Arts & recreation
800	Literature
900	History & geography

Under the main classes are ten *divisions* each (e.g., 150, 370, 790), and each division has ten *sections*, the three-digit numbers. Numbers longer than three digits have a *decimal* or dot after the third. The DDC Summaries (oc .lc/ddc-summaries) provide a high-level overview of all three-digit numbers. There are also six tables (four in abridged editions), whose notation is never used alone, but can be added to many existing numbers to create built numbers.

Works are classified in Dewey by discipline, so it is important to consider the context of a work when deciding where to classify it. A book about costumes, for example, could be in the discipline of customs and folklore (390) or home and family management (640). Users looking for a book on how to make a specific type of costume and users looking for information about the costumes of different cultures may need to look in different places. Students looking for works on American history probably want to start in the 900s but may need to look elsewhere if they want works on a specific topic in American history (e.g., 323 Civil and political rights).

Sometimes, the boundaries between disciplines are clear. How to proceed when they are not? Often, the DDC designates an *interdisciplinary number* for a topic, where a general work belongs. For example, 590 is the interdisciplinary number for animals, so a work that covers animals as pets, on farms, and in zoology would be classified there. Sometimes an interdisciplinary number is given explicitly in a note—for example, at 680 Manufacture of products for specific uses, there is a note "Class here interdisciplinary works on handicrafts." Interdisciplinary numbers are also given in the index. A print version of the index for "First aid" or a browse in WebDewey will show something like figure 8.1:

FIGURE 8.1 | **A WebDewey browse in the Relative Index for "First aid"**

○ Search ◉ Browse First aid		in Relative Index	▾

🔼 **PAGE UP**   🔽 **PAGE DOWN**

Browse Results

Firs--lumber	674.144
First aid	362.18
First aid--health services	362.18
First aid--injuries--medicine	617.10262
First aid--medicine	616.0252

The first heading shown in figure 8.1, which has just "First aid" without any subdivisions, is the interdisciplinary number. The choice of a DDC number should reflect the author's intended use and disciplinary perspective. This means it might still be appropriate to classify an interdisciplinary work in a discipline other than the interdisciplinary number.

The DDC's Introduction (oc.lc/ddc-intro) also outlines several rules for choosing numbers. It is worth looking into all of them, but it is especially worth learning a couple of the more straightforward ones: the "first-of-two rule" and the "rule of three." (Always follow any specific instructions that may appear at a number, however, over these more general rules.)

The "first-of-two" rule says a work that treats two topics equally should be classified in whichever number is given first in the schedules. A work about baseball *and* basketball, for example, would go with basketball in 796.323, not baseball in 796.357. There are some exceptions to this rule (given in the Introduction), but that is the gist of it.

The "rule of three" says a work that treats three or more topics that are part of a broader subject is classified with the broader subject. So a work about the history of Manitoba (971.27), Ontario (971.3), and the Yukon (971.91) would class with the history of Canada at 971.

One potentially valuable resource for determining where to classify a work is the mappings to other classification systems or vocabularies. WebDewey contains certain mappings to *Library of Congress Subject Headings* (LCSH) and *Medical Subject Headings* (MeSH). To classify a work to which LCSH terms have already been assigned, check to see if the Dewey editors have mapped that heading to a specific DDC classification number. Figure 8.2 is an example of mapped LCSH terms in WebDewey, from 641.5 Cooking.

FIGURE 8.2 I **LCSH terms mapped to 641.5 in WebDewey**

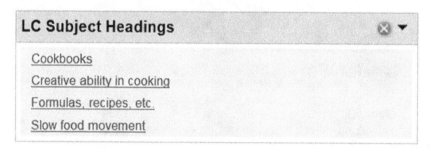

Never make a classification decision based on mappings alone, as they are intended only as starting points.

It can also be helpful to see where others have classified works. Union catalogs such as WorldCat can reveal other libraries' decisions, and resources such as ClassificationWeb provide correlations, showing the frequency with which certain subject headings show up on the same resource as a given DDC number. OCLC also has an experimental research service called Classify (http://classify.oclc.org) that shows how other libraries have classified works. The same caution about mappings applies, although of course this should not be the only consideration. Before using another library's classification decision as an example, make sure that it is actually a good example to follow for a particular situation!

SEGMENTATION

Though OCLC no longer publishes discrete abridged editions of Dewey, the editors continue to supply segmentation marks in numbers. Segmentation marks can be represented by a slash (/) (e.g., 025.3/2) or a prime mark (') (e.g., 025.3'2). The segmentation mark represents a logical place to abridge a number, generally corresponding to the number in previous abridged editions, assuming it is not a more recent number. Consider the example of classifying books on dinosaurs shown in figure 8.3.

FIGURE 8.3 | **567.9 in WebDewey, including upwards and downwards hierarchy and notes**

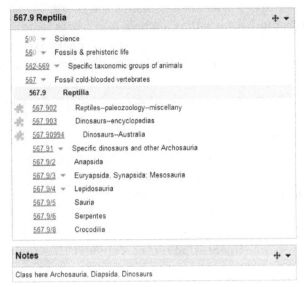

As shown in figure 8.3, a general book about reptiles or dinosaurs is classed with reptiles at 567.9, whether or not the library is abridging numbers. The "class here" note indicates that dinosaurs belong here. Books about specific dinosaurs get more specific numbers, as can be seen in the downwards hierarchy here with 567.91 Specific dinosaurs and other Archosauria. For a book about Stegosaurus or Triceratops, for example, work downwards to 567.915, as shown in figure 8.4.

FIGURE 8.4 | **567.915 in WebDewey, including upwards and downwards hierarchy**

567.915 Stegosauria, Ankylosauria, Ceratopsia (horned dinosaurs)
500   Science
560   Fossils & prehistoric life
562-569   Specific taxonomic groups of animals
567   Fossil cold-blooded vertebrates
567.9   Reptilia
567.91   Specific dinosaurs and other Archosauria
567.912-567.915   Specific dinosaurs
567.915   Stegosauria, Ankylosauria, Ceratopsia (horned dinosaurs)
567.915/3   Stegosaurus
567.915/8   Triceratops

While books on Stegosaurus or Triceratops would have different numbers in a full classification, both would class at 567.915 in an abridged classification, omitting the digits after the segmentation mark. The absence of a segmentation mark, then, means that a whole number is valid for abridged classification. In figure 8.4, that applies to all the numbers except for Stegosaurus and Triceratops. Full and abridged classification are similar to the ideas of *close* (specific) and *broad* classification, respectively, as explained in the Introduction. Note that segmentation marks are not included in call numbers or on shelfmarks.

Segmentation marks represent logical places to truncate a number, but an individual library may have other considerations. Some libraries may limit digits on a spine label to avoid a number being printed across multiple lines. Some may find it useful to segment some numbers but not others—for example, it may make sense to use full classification for works of local history, but abridged classification for others. When deciding whether to abridge differently from WebDewey's segmentation marks, consider this advice from the Introduction about local options:

> Most of the time, the responsibility for implementing an option rests with the local library. Libraries should weigh the value of using an option against the loss in interoperability of numbers. The library will not be able to use numbers assigned by other libraries, and other libraries will not be able to use the optional numbers assigned by the library. In addition, unless the option is widely used in a region, users may be confused by the alternate notation. (oc.lc/ddc-intro)

It is always good practice to record complete DDC numbers in catalog records. This is true for either full or abridged classification; use the MARC 082 field for complete numbers and the 092 field for local numbers (see Appendix: The MARC Format). A library's item-level record, then, can show a different number, such as an abridged or local number.

Ultimately, it is a local decision whether to use full or abridged classification, or a mix of both. The Dewey editors put a lot of thought into what will probably work best for library users, but no one knows users like the staff at a local library!

MIXED CLASSIFICATION

A common local practice for school and public libraries is to have certain sections not classified with Dewey. Dewey's 800s section can give complex notation for world literature, but these libraries often prefer organizing fiction by genre, author's name, or other factors. Similarly, many libraries prefer to collect all biographies in one place, rather than adding T1—092 to Dewey numbers and having them throughout the classification.

There is nothing wrong with such systems. If separating fiction, biography, or other types of works from a main, Dewey-classified collection serves readers, do it! Dewey is a powerful, internationally used classification system, but users' needs should always come first.

NUMBER BUILDING

As of December 2019, the DDC contained over 41,000 assignable numbers. Furthermore, DDC numbers can be built using the tables and other add instructions. There is not an infinite number of potential numbers, but a listing of all of them would still be quite extensive. That is true of abridged classification too, although there are, of course, fewer potential numbers.

Besides the schedules (the numbers 000-999), the full classification has six tables. (Table 3 has three parts: 3A, 3B, and 3C.) The abridged classification has four. Become familiar with Tables 1 and 2, both of which are used very often. Tables 3 and 4 cover literary works and languages, so if the library gets many works in these topics, consider exploring those tables further. Tables 5 and 6 cover specific ethnic/national groups and languages and are not used in the abridged classification.

Table 1 contains *standard subdivisions*, which provide notation that can be added to almost any other Dewey number unless instructed otherwise. Note that one standard subdivision cannot be added to another (again, unless instructed otherwise). Table 1 notation is used to express ideas like "Philosophy and theory" (T1—01) or "Serial publications" (T1—05) that can apply to almost any topic. "History, geographic treatment, biography" is T1—09, and from there, Table 2 notation can be added, which covers specific historical periods and geographic locations. Table 1 is unique in its ability to be used almost anywhere throughout the classification. Never add notation from the other tables unless explicitly instructed to do so in the schedules or tables.

Some of the most common standard subdivisions are noticeable in many assigned built numbers. Almost any number ending in 092 represents biography, such as 796.91/2092, for a biography of a figure skater. A number ending in 0973 (using T2-73) represents the topic in the United States, such as 372.830973, for civics education in the United States.

WebDewey features a number-building tool that can guide users through the sometimes-complex process of building numbers. Built numbers can be saved in WebDewey to be visible in a personal account or at an institution level. They can also be submitted for review by the Dewey editors, where they may be added in WebDewey for all to see.

DDC IN MARC

In a MARC 21 bibliographic-format record, DDC numbers are recorded in field 082. The first indicator of the field expresses whether the number is from the full or abridged classification, and the second indicator expresses whether the number was assigned by the Library of Congress. Always double check and consider the context before accepting a number in copy cataloging.

In the 082 field, $a shows the classification number itself. While this is probably the most important part of the field, it may not be very meaningful without $2, which indicates the edition the number came from. As of 2019, the contents of WebDewey are still considered to be Edition 23. Especially make sure to use $2 if classifying with an older edition, because other catalogers are likely to assume numbers come from the most recent edition. It is good practice to use $2 when adding or updating a number. Even if it has not changed in many editions, it may do so in the future!

Putting it all together, the 082 field in a record for an encyclopedia of dog breeds might look like this:

082 04 $a 636.7/103 $2 23.

This is for a full Dewey number (636.71 Breeds of dogs + T1-03 Dictionaries, encyclopedias, concordances) from the current edition, not assigned by the Library of Congress. Though it should not be part of a library's call number, it is a good idea to include the segmentation mark for others' reference. While the 082 field is repeatable, making it possible to give separate fields for a work's full and abridged numbers, including the segmentation mark in a full number accomplishes much the same thing. A library using full classification would use 636.7103 on such a book, and a library using abridged classification would use 636.7, stopping at the segmentation mark.

A full description of the 082 field is available from the Library of Congress at https://www.loc.gov/marc/bibliographic/bd082.html.

TRANSLATIONS

Though this book is written with North American users in mind, the DDC is used throughout the world. One of its great strengths is its multilingual nature. A work on cars (automobiles) is classified at 388.342, whether they are called cars, *coches*, *biler*, or 汽車. But as a practical matter, classifiers need to be able to read the text of the classification in their own language to effectively use it. The DDC has been translated into many languages, including Arabic, French, German, Greek, Hebrew, Icelandic, Indonesian, Italian, Korean, Norwegian, Russian, Spanish, Swedish, and Vietnamese.

Translators collaborate closely with the Dewey editors, often suggesting improvements or finding errors as they work on their own editions. In some cases, such as Table 2, translations may have more or less developed classifications based on local needs. It is rare that a library in Europe would need notation for each county of each state of the United States, but quite likely that it may want more specific geographic notation for its own country instead, that likewise would not be necessary for American users. Translators and editors still work together to ensure such notation does not conflict.

CONCLUSION

The Dewey Decimal Classification is a powerful, flexible, interoperable way to organize a library's resources. The Dewey editorial team is constantly updating the classification for emerging topics and changes that make it work better. Regular updates on changes, how to use the classification, and even some fun things are posted to the Dewey blog (https://ddc.typepad.com/), usually a few times a month. Editors can be contacted directly at dewey@oclc.org, or direct questions about the Library of Congress's Dewey policy to dewey@loc.gov. An active user community helps make the DDC even better. This makes for a better classification for library users, and that is really what it is all about!

9

CATALOGING FOR CHILDREN IN AN ACADEMIC LIBRARY

RAEGAN WIECHERT | General Cataloger and Assistant Professor
Missouri State University

Academic libraries may seem out of place in a discussion of cataloging for children, but, in fact, there are a couple of settings in which an academic cataloger needs to catalog for children.

The first setting might be called "associated schools," K-12 schools that fall under the administration of a college or university. These may be official laboratory or demonstration schools, or just private schools, especially private religious schools. If cataloging is done independently by associated school librarians, they would make their cataloging decisions as any school librarian would, addressing some considerations if the catalog is shared with an academic library.

If cataloging for these associated schools is done by the academic cataloging department, decisions need to be made that consider the different needs of school-age students versus college students. This means working closely with the school librarian, especially on the classification of materials.

The second setting is the curriculum resource center (CRC). CRCs, also known as instructional or educational resource centers, are collections that support teacher education. They are usually located within the main library or in an education building. These collections are often divided into two sections:

resources for use by teachers/education students (i.e., adults) and resources for use by young students (i.e., children). But it is important to remember that these "children's" resources will mostly be used by adults, and this will affect cataloging decisions.

Regardless of the setup or purpose of these collections, there are some areas and types of materials that need special attention.

SUBJECT AND GENRE HEADINGS

Bibliographic records for children's materials will often reside in a catalog shared by the main academic collection. This means clarifying which items are juvenile and which are not, because many students will not pay attention to pesky things such as the collection where the item resides. One of the most visible methods in such catalogs is the use of juvenile subdivisions (e.g., "Juvenile fiction" or "Juvenile literature") in the subject headings. Not only can K-12 students be taught to look for them, but they can be a red flag to the college students that the item may not meet their needs. For these reasons, it is important to make sure that such headings appear on bibliographic records in an academic library catalog.

If the public catalog is set up to display only *Library of Congress Subject Headings* (LCSH), bibliographic records with only *Library of Congress Children's and Young Adults' Cataloging* (CYAC) headings will need to have regular LCSH added, including the appropriate "juvenile" subdivisions. For example, a record with only a CYAC heading of Pigs—Fiction would not display any subjects in this online catalog. The LCSH Swine—Juvenile fiction needs to be added so that a subject heading will display. If CYAC headings are used in a general library catalog for children's materials, they need to be very clearly marked as such. It may also be worth checking into the efficacy of using two subject heading lists. When two different subject heading lists are used in a library catalog, a user needs to know how and when to search each index for the best results. This can be difficult to convey.

In general, it is easier to use only one subject heading list. Requiring the use of two lists (CYAC for juvenile, LCSH for academic) will be more challenging and time-consuming for the cataloger, not to mention creating a greater likelihood of errors or conflicts. If possible, the catalog in the school library and children's areas should be set to search only the juvenile collections. This may require involving the software providers to adjust the display to highlight the fact the items are juvenile materials. Another possibility in some integrated library systems (ILSs) is to have separate catalogs for adult and children's materials, so that different subject and classification systems could be used without user confusion. However, it should be reiterated that the most common method of showcasing children's material in a catalog that includes adult material is to use adult subject headings with juvenile subdivisions.

In recent years, the acceptance of more genre lists has led to more genre terms being routinely added to records. The use of genre headings, especially for fiction items, can be helpful for students, either in selecting reading materials or in the identification of items for assignments. Please note that although there are some genre headings that identify materials as being for younger audiences (Children's films, Children's audiobooks, etc.), the majority of genre terms are audience-neutral. Unlike LCSH, no subdivisions may be added to genre headings to clarify audience.

CLASSIFICATION

First, a quick discussion about classifications systems. School libraries are almost guaranteed to be using Dewey Decimal Classification (DDC). But the collections in a CRC can be arranged by either Dewey or *Library of Congress Classification* (LCC) or both. By and large, academic catalogers will be using whatever system is already in use, which means that if the library's non-juvenile items are classified in LCC, there is a good chance that the CRC items are also classified using LCC. If this is the case, it may be worth looking into reclassifying the juvenile materials to Dewey. Even though the CRC items are most likely to be used by adults, when those adults become teachers and start working in schools, chances are that the school libraries will be classified using Dewey. Having the children's materials in a CRC classified by Dewey is an appropriate (and necessary) part of the learning environment for future educators.

Academic catalogers will need to work closely with the school librarian to make sure that materials are classified in the best location for the users of that particular school. The librarian should ask such questions as: Do students have to find materials for an assignment that is given annually? Are there yearly topical units (e.g., dinosaurs, political figures) that would benefit from a classification arrangement that easily enables a librarian to pull them out for teacher use or to show to students?

Academic catalogers should also ask questions of the librarian who supervises the CRC. If there is no supervising librarian, the cataloger should contact the library liaison from the Department or College of Education. Are there common assignments that are given to all the education students? Would certain areas benefit from having longer-than-usual call numbers to be better organized? Is there a textbook collection that needs special attention? It is important to work with the host department so the library can better serve the students. Having a library liaison from the education department to help with the collection would result in a more dynamic collection, enhancing the students' educational experience.

For both situations, it might be beneficial to ask if reclassification projects would be useful. Reasons for reclassification would include: part of the collection (e.g., mythology) has grown large and would benefit from having longer numbers so that materials are more subdivided; changes in assignments; changes in the thinking about certain types of materials (special topics, foreign languages, etc.). Ask the CRC supervisor or associated school librarian to keep the cataloging department in the loop about possible big projects. The weeding or reorganization of the collection, or the addition of a large donation will benefit from having a cataloger involved in the process. Advanced notice of large projects also makes it possible to organize other work, so that the cataloging department has the space and time set aside to work on a large project.

SPECIAL FORMATS AND TOPICS

The following cataloging situations could occur in any library that has children's materials. However, they are being discussed here because they are situations that are outside the norm for academic catalogers.

Graphic Novels

Graphic novels can be some of the most popular items in a collection. Their classification and arrangement are therefore of high importance. The recommended Dewey number for graphic novels is 741.5. However, for most graphic novel collections, especially large ones, this one number may not be the best solution. One possibility is to reserve class 741.5 for "classic" graphic novel fiction, such as superheroes and manga, and to interfile other graphic novel fiction in the fiction collection, classified by author. These items could also be shelved in a separate graphic/comic collection and classified by author or series. Nonfiction graphic items could then be classed in the appropriate Dewey classification. Graphic adaptations of novels, plays, fairy tales, and similar works could be classed where the original would be shelved. The integration of graphic materials into the rest of the collection allows for more serendipitous discovery, especially by reluctant readers who might be overwhelmed at the thought of a "regular" book. It also means that nonfiction materials are not divided up simply because a book is formatted a little differently.

The classification option chosen may also depend on the number of graphic novels in a collection. Earlier decisions might need to be revisited if this area experiences rapid growth.

Biographies

Biography is another popular genre for children. In Dewey, there are three basic ways to organize biography: in the 92Xs; adding -092 to topical Dewey numbers; or in a separate B or BIO section. The academic cataloger needs to use the library's established classification choice and not just accept what is on the bibliographic record being used for copy cataloging.

Counting and Alphabet Books

Counting and alphabet books are books for younger children that emphasize numbers or letters, with illustrations that match the emphasized number or letter. These are best gathered under the appropriate Dewey number for counting and the alphabet, rather than scattered throughout the collection by subject or alphabetically by author in the fiction section. For instance, *Counting Puppies and Kittens* would be more appropriately shelved with the other counting books in 513.211 (counting) rather than in 636 (animal husbandry). For *The Construction Alphabet Book*, 421.1 (alphabets in the English language) is a better number (with the other alphabet books) than 690 (construction of buildings). A method that is mostly seen in public libraries, but is also used by school libraries, is to add a sticker with ABC or 123 and then Cutter or alphabetize by author.

Non-English Language Materials

Non-English-language items can be divided into two basic categories: items for the teaching of a non-English language and items that are not in English. The latter category is the one of particular concern. It is not recommended to put all non-English-language materials (both fiction and nonfiction) in one area (e.g., the 400s with languages). However, there are several different classification and shelving options from which to choose. CRCs and schools with mostly English-speaking students might make one decision, whereas a school with large numbers of non-English speakers might make a different one, especially when multiple languages are involved. This is not a decision that should be made solely by the cataloger, but in conjunction with those using or in charge of the collection. The decision should consider not only the population(s) being served, but the intended goals of the collection.

One method is to put non-English fiction in the 400s (based on the item's language), and place nonfiction materials in the appropriate Dewey number. Another, more-preferred method, is to put all items where they would be shelved if they were in English. This allows both English-speaking and non-English readers to easily find information by subject as well as by language, sometimes using one to learn the other. To make interfiled items stand out, a code for the name of the language could be added to the spine label (e.g., SPA 636.8, or FR Dumas). Also, colored stickers could be applied to the book or container spines. If there are one or two languages of a non-English-language collection that need to be emphasized, the items in these languages (both fiction and non-fiction) might be shelved in a special section, apart from the main collection. However, such separation should be carefully considered in terms of the local population. While the separation might help with visibility and browsability, this approach also results in these items being isolated from the rest of the collection. Regardless of the method of shelving used, the resource should be found in the online catalog with a search that is limited by a language facet.

Decisions also need to be made for bilingual items, especially if non-English items are treated differently from the way that English-language items are treated.

Nonbook Items

In recent years, there has been a shift in thinking about the shelving of various nonbook formats. Rather than shelving various media separately, some libraries choose to interfile different formats together on a shelf. For example, nonfiction DVDs and audiobooks might easily be interfiled with the books. For fiction, the audiobooks can be interfiled. Another possibility is setting aside one shelf per section, with all the media for that section on that shelf. These kinds of arrangements can aid browsing and allow for more serendipitous finds, because users may not be aware of the availability of materials in various nonbook formats. Nonstandard items, such as toys, games, kits, and other realia probably should not be interfiled without suitable containers, because their size and shape can cause shelving issues. If interfiling is not a possibility, signage can be used to direct patrons to other relevant resources, locations, or collections.

CONCLUSION

Above all, the thing to remember is to have a dialog with the librarians or faculty members who oversee the collections being cataloged. This way the librarian can make sure that items are arranged in a way that allows for the best use of a particular library's collection, whether it be by education students, faculty, or children.

The next thing to remember is that local need supersedes national standards and rules if these are inadequate. Cataloging children's materials will require more finessing and finagling in both subject headings and classification than in cataloging items for adults.

Finally, it is important to remember that the inclusion of children's materials in an academic library environment is an integral part in the education of future teachers.

10

CATALOGING FOR NON-ENGLISH-SPEAKING CHILDREN AND THEIR FAMILIES

ALLISON G. KAPLAN | Information School
University of Wisconsin–Madison

According to the 2017 United States Census, over 20 percent of households speak a language other than English; and of those, nearly 40 percent speak English "less than well" (U.S. Census 2013-2017). This means there is a good chance that adults using the public library to find books for their children may or may not be comfortable conversing in or reading English. What does that mean for cataloging practice? This chapter is partly collection development, cataloging, and facilities planning, because providing access to information for non-English-speaking patrons in U.S. libraries requires a multipronged approach.

COLLECTION DEVELOPMENT

The needs of the community should be met with inclusion at the forefront of collection development. The question, "Where can I get books in *X* language besides translations of U.S. titles?" pops up every now and then on various discussion lists. While we may indeed want translations of popular U.S. titles, there is value in bringing to library collections books that originated in non-U.S. countries, especially countries represented in the community. To do that, one might need to go beyond the titles available from such vendors as Baker and Taylor, Ingram, or even Amazon. Going "off the list" is one way to expand the collection and to make it more international and, by extension, more familiar to the families being served. However, that may mean purchasing books that do not come with cataloging information, and an original catalog record will need to be created.

One way to keep up with children's books published around the world is to follow the resources provided by IBBY (International Board on Books for Young People), which publishes an annual list of top books (see https://www.ibby.org/awards-activities/awards/ibby-honour-list/ibby-honour-list-2020).

A resource for information about Spanish-language books from Spain and other Latin countries is "America Reads Spanish" (http://americareadsspanish.org/resenas/childrenyoung.html). Here one can see reviews of new books for children and young adults. There is also a list of suggestions for a core collection of Spanish language materials that, while perhaps a little dated (2009), could make for a good starting point (http://americareadsspanish.org/home/essential-guide-to-spanish-reading.html).

Additionally, remember the power of the wordless picture book. Books without words can encourage non-English-language speaking adults to connect with their children through "reading" these books in their own language. IBBY has a list titled "silent books" that was created first to address the literacy needs of refugee populations on the Italian island of Lampedusa but continues today as an international resource (www.ibby.org/awards-activities/activities/silent-books/?L=0). The Reading Rockets initiative website includes a database of books that can be searched by "wordless" (https://www.readingrockets.org/bookfinder). The Library of Congress and Sears subject headings utilize the phrase "Stories without words," which can be used to check the library catalog for these types of books already in the collection.

CATALOGING

The rules for cataloging non-English-language materials are the same as those for cataloging English-language materials. However, issues arise with some fields in the MARC format that require attention for translations or other non-English-language materials. This section covers recommendations when creating original catalog records.

Coded MARC Field 041

The 041 field for multiple languages or translations provides coding for the original language of the item along with the translated language, or for items in multiple languages. If the item is in one language and is not a translation, do not use this field. In this field, pay attention to the indicators: use the first indicator to show if the item is a translation ("1") or is not a translation ("0").

For example, *El gato ensombrerado* is a Spanish language translation of the book *The Cat in the Hat,* which was originally published in English. In this case, use the 041 field with a first indicator value of "1." The first subfield will be "a" for the language of the text and a second subfield "h" for the language of the original text. Using this example: 041 1_ $a spa $h eng (the item is a translation from English into Spanish).

Movies with multiple soundtracks are not treated as translations. However, a movie with a soundtrack in one language and captions in another is considered a translation. For example, the 041 field for a movie in Korean with English subtitles would look like this:

> 041   1_ $a kor $j eng

Watch out for adaptations of text in other languages. For example, the BabyLit board book *Anna Karenina: A Fashion Primer* is an English-language adaptation of the book originally published in Russian. However, the text is so changed from the original version that it is not treated as a translation of the original work. For details on the 041 field, see www.loc.gov/marc/bibliographic/bd041.html.

Other Fields in the MARC Record

As described in chapter 4, "Cataloging Children's Materials Using RDA," record the title and statement of responsibility as it appears on the title page in the 245 field. Thus, an example of a book in English would look like this:

> 245   10 $a Pete the cat treasury : $b five groovy stories / $c Kimberly & James Dean.

If a title is in two languages, as with a bilingual resource, transcribe the first title first, followed by an equal sign (=) prior to the subfield "b" information. Avoid the temptation to record an English-language title first if it is not displayed first on the title page. Use the 246 field (Varying form of title) to record the title in the second language. An example of a bilingual book in English and Chinese would be:

245   10 $a Which way? = $b Na ge fang xiang? / $c created by Bev
               Schumacher ; graphic design, Bev Kirk.
246   31 $a Na ge fang xiang?

The 246 field indicators are different from those in the 245 field. The first indicator of the 246 field is used for generating notes in the catalog record. There are several values for this first indicator and, in this example, the value "3" means that the title will be added to the catalog without any further notes in the catalog record. The second indicator of the 246 field defines the type of title being entered. In the example above, "Na ge fang xiang?" is a parallel title, thus the value "1" is used. The 246 field's filing indicators do not code for initial articles, which the second indicator of the 245 field does. For parallel titles with initial articles, drop the initial article in the 246 field. As seen in the example above, the 246 field includes only the alternate title; it does not include the statement of responsibility and does not end in a period (except in the given example, it must end with the punctuation included in the title).

When working with translated items, the catalog record needs to include a reference to the title in its original language, which is referred to as the "preferred title" in RDA rules and as the "uniform title" in AACR2. For the purposes of this chapter, this form of title will be referred to as the preferred title. The preferred title for a translated work appears in the 240 field. The best approach for creating the information that will appear in this field is to search the Library of Congress Authorities database (https://authorities.loc .gov). If the title is not in the Authorities database, try searching WorldCat (https://www.worldcat.org/), where the preferred title should be provided in the line "Other Titles." If that too fails, then a 240 field must be created without help from the experts. The first indicator code indicates whether or not the uniform title will be displayed in the record. To display the uniform title, use the code number "1." The second indicator is used for non-filing characters just as seen in the discussion for the 245 field in chapter 4. Practices for including or dropping initial articles in the 240 field vary. When following Library of Congress practice, do not include the initial article in the 240 field and use the code number "0" for all uniform titles. For example, following this rule, *The Cat in the Hat* would become *Cat in the hat* in the 240 field. For more information about using authority records, see chapter 5. Note also that older records and some cataloging systems may refer to the preferred title as the uniform title.

The preferred title is entered in the subfield "a." Additionally, include a subfield "l" [lowercase L] for the language of the translation, writing out the name of the language. Here is an example of the Spanish language version of *Clifford to the Rescue*:

```
100  1_    $a Bridwell, Norman.
240  10    $a Clifford to the rescue. $l Spanish
245  10    $a Clifford al rescate / $c Norman Bridwell ; traducido por Teresa
           Mlawer.
700  1_    $a Mlawer, Teresa, $e translator.
```

In this example, the 700 field is used to provide access for the name of the translator.

Use the note field 546 to highlight language aspects of the item. For example,

```
546  _ _    $a In Spanish.
546  _ _    $a Text is in English and Spanish.
```

If the information is available, or if you or someone in your library or community is fluent in the language of the item, add a second summary statement (520 field) in the language of the item. This provides for more equitable access to information in the catalog. Be careful about using translating programs such as Google Translate or Microsoft Translator to create summary statements in other languages. Those translation programs may not always account for nuances in language and often produce simply a transliteration rather than a true translation of text.

Classification in and of itself is not a special issue except when the materials are shelved in a special area. Non-English-language materials are often organized in a special "world languages" (avoid the phrase "foreign languages") section, making those materials very easy to find. However, consider aspects of inclusion. Would it be more inclusive for the non-English-speaking patron needing books about dogs to go to the dog section, find materials in their native language, and look at English-language materials as well? In that case, would the materials be used more frequently than if they were shelved in a separate section? If the community is mostly non-English-speaking, what is the message being sent by separating the materials? These are questions to consider in classifying materials.

When possible, create subject headings in the language of the item. Bilingual thesauri can be helpful here. For Spanish, see the fourth edition of *Subject Headings for School and Public Libraries*, which is a Latin American translation of LCSH and CYAC terms. Another helpful resource is *SALSA de Tópicos/ Subjects in SALSA: Spanish and Latin American Subject Access* by Miller and Arellano, which not only presents information about subject access but also argues for the importance of bilingual access.

The final cataloging recommendation: involve community members! Part of capacity building in communities includes asking for help in processing these materials. Using a guide to transliterate materials that do not use the Roman alphabet, such as Arabic or Russian (see https://www.loc.gov/catdir/cpso/roman.html) may be fine for physical description of an item; however, when it comes to providing access through summary statements or subject headings, getting help from a community member may prove invaluable.

SIGNAGE

This final section addresses the issue that could really be the most helpful of all: signage. When thinking about access to information, it isn't enough just to have signs on the outside windows. Once multilingual community members come in, they need to feel welcomed on the inside of the library as well as on the outside. The "Libraries Are For Everyone" movement provides the impetus for increased signage. Here is a challenge: walk into the library and pretend that you speak English "less than well" (as the United States Census identifies it). What is your first impression? Can you easily find the children's section? No? How can that be made more identifiable? Once in the children's section, can you find the books about dogs and cats? No? How can that be fixed? The list goes on and on. Using photos or other graphics can help create a welcoming space for all community members.

Be careful about color choices for the signs. Talking with community members can help in choosing colors. There are also business sites on the web that can be useful, such as K International's, *The Language Blog* (https://www.k-international.com/blog/color-meanings-around-the-world/); or Xerox International Color Guide (https://www.xerox.com/en-us/small-business/tips/color-guide).

CONCLUSION

Libraries should reflect and embrace the communities they serve. This applies as much to the materials collected and the way those materials are cataloged as it does to services being provided. Being more inclusive in collection development presents a golden opportunity to empower community members by encouraging suggestions for items for the collection as well as suggestions for ways to provide access to all items.

When buying materials "off the list" that have no cataloging copy available, create records using current cataloging standards for translated and multilingual aspects. Providing bilingual access to materials through the library catalog when possible, and when authoritative translations can be provided, is a big step in creating a completely inclusive library.

RESOURCES

America Reads Spanish. http://americareadsspanish.org.

Bristow, Barbara A., ed. *Sears List of Subject Headings.* Ipswich, MA: H. W. Wilson/ Grey House Publishing, 2018.

Calimano, Iván E., and Ageo García, eds. *Sears: Lista de Encabezamientos de Materia: Nueva Traducción y Adaptación de la Lista Sears.* New York: H. W. Wilson, 2008.

Fountain, Joanna F. *Subject Headings for School and Public Libraries,* bilingual fourth ed. Santa Barbara, CA: Libraries Unlimited, 2012.

IBBY (International Board on Books for Young People). www.ibby.org/?L=0.

K International. *The Language Blog.* Available at https://www.k-international.com/ blog/color-meanings-around-the-world/.

Libraries Are For Everyone. Available at https://hafuboti.com/. At the time of publication, this website was under construction and this link may not be viable.

Miller, David P., and Arellano F. Martínez. *SALSA de Tópicos=Subjects in SALSA: Spanish and Latin American Subject Access.* Chicago: Association for Library Collections and Technical Services, 2007.

Reading Rockets Bookfinder. https://www.readingrockets.org/bookfinder.

United States Census Bureau. *2013-2017 American Community Survey 5-Year Estimates.* https://data.census.gov/cedsci/table?q=language&tid=ACSST 1Y2018.S1601&hidePreview=false

Xerox. *International Color Guide.* https://www.xerox.com/en-us/small-business/ tips/color-guide.

Library of Congress Cataloging Resources:

Country codes for coding for specific geographic information: www.loc.gov/ marc/geoareas/gacs_name.html.

Language codes for coding for the language of the item: www.loc.gov/marc/ languages/language_name.html.

MARC Bibliographic information for specific field information: www.loc.gov/ marc/bibliographic/.

Romanization tables: https://www.loc.gov/catdir/cpso/roman.html.

CHILDREN'S SEARCHING BEHAVIOR

Implications for Cataloging

LESLEY S. J. FARMER
California State University Long Beach

"The library is dumb. It doesn't have anything on cars."
"How come I can't find a magazine article in the library catalog?"
"Where can I get something on Mike Angelo? It's not coming up on the library's computer."

These comments may sound familiar to librarians who work with young people. Every day new children come through the door—or the library web portal—and can't figure out how the library "works."

These young users just want to find the information, but that quest involves several factors: the information seeker's characteristics, the information task's characteristics, the domain's characteristics, the system's characteristics, and the contextual environment and situation. When focusing on using library catalogs, young people need to know how to:

- translate an information need into a searchable query
- create and carry out a query for a given information retrieval system (i.e., language use)
- successfully use online resources

These competencies may be problematic for children because of developmental limitations (e.g., the ability to abstract and generalize information) and lack of instruction and experience. In comparison to adults, children plan less and wander more, browse and search equally often, favor interactivity over preplanning, scroll pages less, recover, find workarounds to search obstacles, and take more time to complete the task successfully. Among children, their information-seeking behavior varies by age, grade level, motor skills, language knowledge, reading ability, metacognitive ability, domain knowledge and vocabulary, online experience, and type of source. Finding information for an open-ended task is usually more successful than searching for factual information, mainly because the former offers more options for relevant answers. Another significant factor for success is the quality of the library catalog or integrated learning management system.

Library access tools such as online catalogs are designed to be used independently, but the developers are adults who generally do not have children as their target users. Children are likely to explore through trial and error until they feel successful—or until they feel frustrated; some will just switch to a more familiar or easier topic (Guinee, Eagleton, and Hall 2003). Children seldom use the "help" function, if available, and most children do not ask for human help.

Even if young searchers get some kind of results when querying a catalog, they might not know what to do with those results. Children are likely to click on the title (usually displayed prominently), which usually results in fuller citation information and sometimes the full text or directions to access the full text. Without instruction, children are unlikely to understand call numbers, for instance. New integrated learning management systems with discovery search incorporate commercial databases into the mix of resources and broaden the possible research results, but children are unlikely to differentiate between the kinds of resources. Nor do children typically know how to use filtering features such as date range or resource type to refine their search; thus, they may get an overload of hits.

Knowing how children seek information, librarians should make sure that catalogs themselves display simple screencasts and provide visual guide sheets with examples, because library workers might not be available to help at the time of need. More fundamentally, though, software designers need to create online catalogs with input from youth-serving librarians and young users as early as possible in the production process. At the very least, administrators who decide which online catalog program to acquire should have youth-serving librarians and young users pilot-test the potential program first for its ease of use. More specific recommendations follow.

- Provide related kid-friendly terms along with standard subject headings.
- Provide summaries and keyword-searchable analytic notes, which might not be included in purchased catalog records.
- Confirm that subject headings follow standard subject heading lists such as the *Sears List, Library of Congress Subject Headings* (LCSH), or *Library of Congress Children's Subject Headings* (CSH). Include both specific and general subject headings (e.g., Collies and Dogs).
- Make sure that series titles are included.
- Provide both searching and browsing options.
- Provide question prompts to help children refine their search strategies.
- Provide the option to document the search strategy history.
- Include a spell-check/approximation feature (e.g., if a child types in "kat," the program asks: "Do you mean cat?").
- Support a natural language interface.
- Provide content-specific help or pop-up dialogue boxes that appear when the user clicks on a page's "Need help?" button.

RESOURCES

Bilal, D. "Research on Children's Information Seeking on the Web." *Youth Information-Seeking Behavior: Theories, Models, and Issues* 1 (2004): 39-50.

Chelton, M., and C. Cool. *Youth Information-Seeking Behavior.* Lanham, MD: Scarecrow Press, 2007.

Guinee, K., Maya B. Eagleton, and Tracey. E. Hall. "Adolescents' Internet Search Strategies: Drawing upon Familiar Cognitive Paradigms when Accessing Electronic Information Sources." *Journal of Educational Computing Research* 29, no. 3 (2003), 363-74.

Todd, R. J. "Theme Section: Adolescents of the Information Age: Patterns of Information Seeking and Use, and Implications for Information Professionals." *School Libraries Worldwide* 9, no. 2 (2003), 27-46.

THE FUTURE OF CATALOGING FOR CHILDREN

MICHELE ZWIERSKI | Manager, Cataloging Services
Nassau Library System
Uniondale, New York

"It's tough to make predictions, especially about the future"—YOGI BERRA

As technology soars ahead, there is competition to capture consumers. Whatever the latest commercial trends are, libraries seek to introduce cutting-edge experiences to their community in a no-cost (or low-cost) manner. Looking back, some "cutting-edge" materials have included DVDs, compact discs, e-books, and videogames. Today these materials are commonly found in library collections. Even discarded formats come back again, like the current interest in vinyl records. Libraries are also expanding the definition of what a collection should contain. They are purchasing and circulating musical instruments, seeds, clothing, museum passes, Wi-Fi hotspots, and other nontraditional library materials. Collections are constantly being reshaped to stay current and relevant in today's world.

Children's collections, whether stand-alone or as part of a larger library collection, are also subject to these larger library trends. Children today (known as Generation Z, or Gen Z) are technologically savvy, having been born into a world already comfortable with the internet. It makes sense that children's collections embrace technology and use it as part of a wider educational journey. Collections should include both the familiar and the unknown. Users, especially children, should feel the comfort of materials familiar to them, like beloved books and known formats. Library users also should feel the excitement and pull of new library materials, like new formats, titles, and authors.

Parents and educators continue to have high expectations of children's collections. Parents need reputable materials of the highest standards. Educators need materials to support classroom activities. Everyone wants materials in languages spoken in the community. Librarians, sensitive to community needs, build collections that support and inspire everyone, children included.

When purchasing new materials or starting new services, libraries rely, in part, on marketing to stir interest and usage. The online catalog is a subtle but concrete marketing tool. What better way to promote a library than to have an inventory of what the library owns, whether it is available, and information on where to get it, as shown in the library's online catalog? Catalogers have an opportunity to support a library mission, piece by piece, bibliographic record by bibliographic record.

Catalogers always have one foot in the past and one foot in the future. They maintain legacy catalogs while implementing new standards and adding new technologies. Catalogers know how the online catalog works and have strategies for successful discovery of materials. When a library begins new services and purchases new materials, a cataloger should be able to market these to the community through bibliographic records that are thoughtful, sharp, detailed, and complete, including as many appropriate keywords as possible.

THE FUTURE OF CATALOGING

Because it is difficult to predict what new materials will be available for consumers and library collections, it is best to remain open and creative with respect to acquisition and cataloging. Follow the existing rules and follow a cataloger's instinct. Be sure to create records that can blend into the existing catalog yet reflect the substance and nature of the new resource.

The ritual of cataloging is being reshaped. There is a yearning for library resources to be discovered online via a searcher's daily internet experience. So instead of conceptualizing a catalog as being mainly used as a local inventory of descriptive records, current library cataloging thought is focusing on identifying relationships among resources.

The new cataloging rules, RDA, have been designed with a new architecture in mind, one that can express relationships in a more contemporary, shareable environment. With this prospect, the MARC format is showing its limitations. BIBFRAME is the current data model that is being developed to replace the MARC format.

The real test of any innovation is how that innovation responds to daily common use. Unfortunately for cataloging, the true test would be using these new dynamic bibliographic records in an online catalog. Most available integrated library systems (ILSs) do not have the ability to store, index, retrieve, and display records in non-MARC format (including BIBFRAME). In order to move forward, commercial vendors need to provide flexible platforms that allow for the testing and use of these new records.

Catalogers face the challenging and exciting task of keeping a catalog functioning while cataloging rules are changing and while librarians are redefining what collections (and catalogs) should include. It is not easy to be proactive. When cataloging rules change, it is difficult to anticipate the impact on a local library operation. Not all new resources end up becoming part of a library collection, where they demand the attention of catalogers. When the time and opportunity arrive, embrace change and make it work.

It's not always easy (or convenient) to find current information on cataloging trends. Look for articles in current journals. If bibliographic records are downloaded from a vendor, look for anything different. Ask the vendor about any changes. From time to time, search on the internet for current cataloging topics, like "library cataloging trends" or "RDA school libraries." As with any internet searches, results may include relevant articles, presentations, or documentation. If possible, attend meetings, workshops, and webinars, and don't be shy about contacting the authors of any material that is of interest.

As with anything in a library work setting, there will be surprises, disappointments, and compromises. A catalog can be the perfect environment to call the future of library service to the attention of users. Catalogers have the knowledge and heart to make discovery a reality and set the stage for a current, relevant, and exciting library experience.

RESOURCE

"Future Organization of Things." *OLA Quarterly* 25, no. 1 (2019). https://doi.org/10.7710/1093-7374.25.01.

APPENDIX: THE MARC FORMAT

MICHELE ZWIERSKI | Manager, Cataloging Services
Nassau Library System
Uniondale, New York

The collection of a library is searchable through a library OPAC. When typing in a search, a user can choose to limit the query in several different ways. For example, if the author is known, the searcher can select a name search for the OPAC to search only in the name indexes for the author. When a search result is displayed, as shown in figure A.1, further "refining" can be done. A user can check the "facet" boxes for reducing the number of records in the display. For example, a title search of "moby dick" can result in a large number of "hits." If a user is only interested in a new book in English, a format facet of *book,* a language facet of *English*, and a date facet of *2019* can be activated.

All these searching choices are made possible by the correct tagging of the cataloging record information. That is done through use of the MARC format.

MARC (MAchine-Readable Cataloging) is a set of standards developed in the 1960s as a method of tagging cataloging records (i.e., bibliographic records) for use in computers. Most online library catalogs exclusively use records that are in the MARC format. When the bibliographic records are in the same format and the individual records are correctly tagged, the ILS can then index and display the information successfully.

FIGURE A.1 | **OPAC view of title search results for *Moby Dick***

When working with bibliographic records that are in a library catalog (or are about to be imported into the library catalog) it is important to check records for correct tagging, especially the codes that directly drive the discovery process.

When a library resource is cataloged and a bibliographic record is being created, the record content is then tagged and separated into fields and subfields. Authority records are also coded in the MARC format, so that these work records can exist and perform within a library catalog. See chapter 5, "Looking at Authority Records," for further information and examples.

The most-used fields will be discussed below. A more complete listing (including definitions and examples) of MARC 21 (the most current version) is available at https://www.loc.gov/marc/.

Figure A.2 is a partial example from an ILS. Note that each different ILS may display the MARC record differently.

In figure A.2, MARC 21 field three-digit tags are listed in the first number data column and field "indicators" are in the next (two-digit) column. The third column begins the "variable" field with information separated into coded subfields. In some ILSs, this third column begins with subfield code "a." In most library online catalogs, this subfield "a" in any field is implied and not entered or displayed.

The variable fields are further subdivided in smaller fields, called subfields. The subfields contain specific elements of each area of information. In MARC,

FIGURE A.2 | **MARC record example**

008 _ _ 180316s2019 nyu c   000 1 eng

010 _ _ 2018005488

020 _ _ 9781524718886 $q (trade)

020 _ _ 9781524718893 $q (lib. bdg.)

040 _ _ DLC $b eng $c DLC $e rda $d DLC

050 0 0 PZ7.C446265 $b One 2019

082 0 0 [Fic] $2 23

100 1 _ Choldenko, Gennifer, $d 1957- $e author.

245 1 0 One-third nerd / $c Gennifer Choldenko ; illustrations by Églantine Ceulemans.

264 1 _ New York : $b Wendy Lamb Books, an imprint of Random House Children's Books, $c [2019]

300 _ _ 211 pages ; $c 22 cm

336 _ _ text $2 rdacontent

337 _ _ unmediated $2 rdamedia

338 _ _ volume $2 rdacarrier

520 _ _ Ten-year-old Liam and his two younger sisters, precocious third-grader Dakota and second-grader Izzy, who has Down syndrome, face the possibility of losing their beloved dog, Cupcake, who keeps urinating on their apartment's carpet.

650 _ 1 Brothers and sisters $v Fiction.

650 _ 1 Family life $v Fiction.

650 _ 1 German shepherd dog $v Fiction.

650 _ 1 Dogs $v Fiction.

650 _ 0 Brothers and sisters $v Juvenile fiction.

650 _ 0 Families $v Juvenile fiction.

650 _ 0 German shepherd dog $v Juvenile fiction.

700 1 _ Ceulemans, Eglantine, $e illustrator.

each subfield also uses a code. Because these codes can be numbers or letters, a symbol (or delimiter) is used to differentiate the code from the actual data content. For example:

    245   1 0   Medusa's web : $b a novel

The subfield "b" precedes the subtitle "a novel." A delimiter, in this example, is represented by a dollar sign. Neither the dollar sign nor the "b" is part of the book subtitle. Delimiters can look different in different systems. Some examples of delimiter characters are "$", "|" or "‡" In a public catalog, neither the delimiter nor the subfield name are displayed. Any spaces typed before the delimiter or after the subfield code convert to a single space when the bibliographic record is entered or displayed. In this chapter, a space is inserted before and after the delimiter and the subfield code just to make the examples easier to use.

In figure A.2, the Author field (100 field) contains the name of the author of the book, Gennifer Choldenko. The information is given in a structured form. The beginning of the field ($a; the $a is usually understood) contains the author's last name, comma, first name and other identifying elements. The $d is defined in the 100 field as dates associated with the name. It's important to know that each subfield is defined for the field in which it is contained. A $c in the Title field (245) means "statement of responsibility," whereas a $c in the Publication field (264) means the "date of publication."

Although the entire MARC record should be coded correctly, there are some fields that are critical and feed directly into the facets used by the ILS. Some of these basic fields are language, format, and title.

There are several control fields available for use. In figure A.2, there is control field 008. This control field contains pieces of data usually used by the ILS for limiting options. This 008 has (among other truncated information) a publication date and a language code ("eng"). These elements can also be used by an ILS as facets for narrowing a search.

Format is another piece of MARC data that should be checked. Different ILS systems expose (and extract) this information in different ways. In figure A.3, "Format" is shown in this ILS cataloging module at the top of the MARC record as Material Type:

FIGURE A.3 | **OPAC View of Fixed Field Code for Material Type**

Language	eng English		Cat. Date	12-14-2020		Bib Code 3	J BWHERE
Skip	0		Bib Level	m MONOGRAPH		Country	nyu New York (State)
Location	none		Material Type	a BOOK			

Some valid codes for this field are defined in the MARC format as shown below (a full list is available at https://www.loc.gov/marc/bibliographic/).

 a for Language material (books)
 c for Printed music (musical scores)
 g for Projected medium (like DVDs and Blu-rays)

A local system may have additional assigned codes that are defined and valid at a local level.

The title field (245) contains the title as it appears on the title page. In most languages, a title can begin with an initial article. When an initial article begins the title, it is coded as not to be indexed ("ignored" or "skipped"). For example, for the title "The book with no pictures," the first significant word of the title is "book." If coded correctly (with a field 245 second indicator of "4" counting 3 for the number of letters in "the" and one for the space after it), this title will index with other materials whose titles begin with "Book" as opposed to indexing with other materials having the title beginning with the word "The."

If a catalog search for known material is unsuccessful, the explanation may lie in the MARC coding for that record. Knowing common suspect areas and knowing how to fix errors is an important skill to have as librarian.

For more MARC information, see another Library of Congress resource, "Understanding MARC bibliographic" (https://www.loc.gov/marc/umb/). This is an older resource and does not include all the current MARC tags available, but the explanatory and history sections are excellent. For current information (and instruction) on MARC 21 visit https://www.loc.gov/marc/bibliographic/.

Another good source of definitions and examples of MARC tags is the OCLC resource *Bibliographic Formats and Standards* (https://www.oclc.org/bibformats/en.html).

MOST-USED MARC FIELDS FOR BIBLIOGRAPHIC RECORDS

This list is not comprehensive. For a full set of MARC tags and codes, with definitions and examples, visit https://www.loc.gov/marc/bibliographic/.

When "speaking" in MARC (as listed below), an "x" in the field tag (like 5xx) means any field that begins with the number 5. "5xx" represents all numbers between 500 and 599. "33x" represents all numbers between 330 and 339.

Some fields (and subfields) can be repeated.

Using figure A.2 (when appropriate):

010   **Library of Congress Control Number (LCCN)**

A unique number assigned to a MARC record by the Library of Congress.

010   _ _   2018005488

020   **International Standard Book Number (ISBN)**

A numeric number assigned to commercially released material. The number was expanded from ten digits to thirteen digits in 2007. The number is intended to be unique. It may be printed on a resource with hyphens. Do not include the hyphens when entering this number into a MARC record.

020   _ _   9781524718886

040   **Cataloging source**

This field identifies the library that created the bibliographic record. A librarian can quickly identify records that are of high quality or are most likely to be compatible with a local catalog. A list of the codes and definitions is located at https://www.loc.gov/marc/organizations/.

040   _ _   DLC $b eng $e rda $c DLC

Translation: The Library of Congress cataloged and entered this bibliographic record. Use of this record is intended for English-language catalogs and was cataloged using rules from RDA (Resource Description and Access).

050   **Library of Congress Classification Number**

Locally assigned LC call numbers are tagged in most systems as 090.

082   **Dewey Decimal Classification Number**

Locally assigned Dewey call numbers are tagged in most systems as 092.

Subfield 2 indicates the edition of Dewey used in the creation of this number. This number was created based on the 23rd edition (the last available print edition).

082   _   [Fic] $2 23

082   _ _   636.737/4 $2 23

100   **Name entry: Personal name**

Subfields: $d dates associated with the name

$e relator terms

A relator term can be assigned to a name heading to describe the "relationship" between the name and the material being cataloged. The list of authorized terms (along with definitions) is available at https://www.loc .gov/marc/relators/relaterm.html.

100   1 _   Choldenko, Gennifer, $d 1957- $e author.

245   **Title statement**

Indicators: The first indicator: 0 = No added entry ; 1 = Added entry

If the record has a 1xx field, the first indicator will be 1. If the record has no 1xx field, the first indicator will be 0. The second indicator is a filing indicator.

Subfields: $b remainder of title (including parallel titles and subtitles)

$c statement(s) of responsibility

245   1 0   One-third nerd / $c by Gennifer Choldenko ; illustrations by Eglantine Ceulemans.

245   1 0   Animal 123 : $b one to ten and back again / $c illustrated by Kate Sheppard.

245   1 4   The festival of bones = $b El festival de las calaveras / $c Luis San Vicente ; translation by John William Byrd & Bobby Bird.

246   **Varying form of title**

Indicators will specify forms and locations of the variant title(s) (see MARC 21).

246   3 _   1/3 nerd

264   **Production, publication, distribution, manufacture, and copyright notice**

Indicators: The first indicator is always blank.

The second indicator will indicate the function of the entity in $b.

Subfields: $a   Place

$b   Name of entity

$c   Date

264   _ 1   New York : $b Wendy Lamb Books, an imprint of Random House Children's Books, $c [2019]

300   **Physical description**

Indicators: Both blank

Subfields: $a   Extent of item (number of pages, volumes, etc.)

$b   Other physical details (illustrations)

$c   Dimensions (size)

300   _ _   211 pages : $b illustrations ; $c 22 cm.

33x   **Content/Media/Type**

With the introduction of RDA, new fields were created to allow more specific descriptions of the material being cataloged. For a list of the identifying codes (with definitions) see http://www.loc .gov/standards/valuelist/.

336   Content type

337   Media type

338   Carrier type

336   _ _   text $2 rda content

336   _ _   still image $2 rda content

337   _ _   unmediated $2 rda media

338   _ _   volume $2 rda carrier

490   **Series statement (as it appears on the item)**

Indicators: First: 0   Series is not traced (i.e., indexed)

First: 1   Series is traced (or is traced differently) (used together with 8xx)

Subfields: $v   Series numbering

5xx   **Note fields**

There are many notes that can be added to a cataloging entry. A complete list of the 5xx fields, indicators and subfields is available at https://www.loc.gov/marc/bibliographic/.

Some of the indicators in the 5xx fields automatically display a display constant. In the example below of a 520 field, the first indicator is blank. This will trigger a display constant of "Summary:" to display before the actual note when displayed in the public catalog. For this field, a cataloger does not have to type in the word Summary before the note. A correct first indicator of blank will trigger the word Summary to appear in front of the 520 field in the public catalog.

MARC record:

520   _ _   Ten-year-old Liam and his two younger sisters, precocious third-grader Dakota and second-grader Izzy, who has Down syndrome, face the possibility of losing their beloved dog, Cupcake, who keeps urinating on their apartment's carpet.

Public Catalog display:

Summary: Ten-year-old Liam and his two younger sisters, precocious third-grader Dakota and second-grader Izzy, who has Down syndrome, face the possibility of losing their beloved dog, Cupcake, who keeps urinating on their apartment's carpet.

Some of the most common for children's materials:

505   Contents note

520   Summary

521   Target audience note (a first indicator of "1" defines the note to contain "Interest age level")

586   Awards note

520   _ _   Ten-year-old Liam and his two younger sisters, precocious third-grader Dakota and second-grader Izzy, who has Down syndrome, face the possibility of losing their beloved dog, Cupcake, who keeps urinating on their apartment's carpet.

521   1 _   Ages 8-12

6xx   **Subject access fields**

600   Name used as subject

650   Topical subject term

655   Index term / Genre form

The second indicator defines what thesaurus (or subject heading list) was used for these controlled headings.

Second indicators (most common):

_ 0   Library of Congress

_ 1   LC subject headings for children's literature (CYAC headings)

_ 7   Source of heading identified in $2 of the 6xx field (in this example, FAST headings).

(Other source subject heading lists include *Sears*, BISAC, and *Hennepin*)
For further advice about using the 6xx fields, see chapter 6.

Example from one record:

650   _ 1   Brothers and sisters $v Fiction.

650   _ 1   Family life $v Fiction.

650   _ 1   German shepherd dog $v Fiction.

650   _ 1   Down syndrome $v Fiction.

650   _ 0   Brothers and sisters $v Juvenile fiction.

650   _ 0   Families $v Juvenile fiction.

650   _ 0   German shepherd dog $v Juvenile fiction.

650   _ 0   Down syndrome $v Juvenile fiction.

655   _ 7   Down syndrome. $2 fast $0 (OCoLC)fst00897227

655   _ 7   Fiction. $2 fast $0 (OCoLC)fst1423787

655   _ 7   Juvenile works. $2 fast $0 (OCoLC)fst01411637

7xx   **Added entry fields**

Important names associated with the item: additional authors, editors, illustrators, cast members, narrators, etc. Subfields are the same that can be used in the 1xx fields, including (in this example), the $e (relator code).

700   1 _   Ceulemans, Eglantine, $e illustrator

800-830   **Series statement traced differently (than as it appears on the item)**

490   1 _   Hilo ; $v book 5

800   1 _   Winick, Judd. $t Hilo ; $v bk. 5

In conclusion, cataloging records are in the MARC format. A librarian familiar with this standard will be able to create a consistent, successful online catalog, identify and correct display errors, and communicate with vendors on data exchange and data cleanup projects.

BIBLIOGRAPHY OF SELECTED RESOURCES

RAEGAN WIECHERT | Assistant Professor and Cataloger
Missouri State University with CCK6 Editors

MAJOR INTEGRATED LIBRARY SYSTEM (ILS) VENDORS

Evergreen (https://evergreen-ils.org/)
A free open source ILS.

ExLibris (https://www.exlibrisgroup.com/ and https://www.iii.com/)
Alma is the current iteration, but many libraries still use Aleph and Voyager.
ExLibris owns Innovative Interfaces, which was a separate company until
2019. The current iteration available from Innovative Interfaces is Sierra,
although some libraries still use Millennium. It also offers Polaris, which was
previously a separate system.

FOLIO (https://www.folio.org/)
An open-source library services platform (LSP) launched for early adopters
in 2020.

Follett (https://www.follettlearning.com/technology/products/library
-management-system).
The ILS used by most school libraries; the iteration current in 2020 was
Follett Destiny.

Koha (https://koha-community.org/)
> A free open source ILS.

OCLC (https://www.oclc.org/en/worldshare-management-services.html)
> WorldShare Management Services is a cloud-based discovery platform that includes a local ILS.

SirsiDynix (https://www.sirsidynix.com/)
> Symphony is the current iteration, although many libraries still use its Horizon product.

TIND (https://info.tind.io/ILS)
> One of the newest open-source, cloud-based ILSs, not yet in wide use.

TLC (https://tlcdelivers.com/library-solution/)
> Current products are CARL X, CARL Connect, and Library Solution, which are used mainly by public and school libraries.

SOURCES FOR MARC RECORDS

Most vendors of e-resources and many vendors of other resources provide MARC records for the items they sell. E-resource records are usually included as part of the purchase price, but records for other types of items often entail an additional charge. However, it should be noted that the quality of these records can range from excellent to abysmal. Sample records from new vendors should be carefully reviewed before importing into an ILS. If there is no choice of source, poor records should be modified before they are imported in order to avoid problems and cleanup at the local level.

BookWhere Online (www.webclarity.info/products/bookwhere-online/)
> A subscription web-based search and copy-cataloging tool.

Library of Congress (https://www.loc.gov/z3950/#lc; https://www.loc.gov/z3950/lcserver.html)
> Bibliographic and authority records are available for free download through the Z39.50 protocol.

Midwest Library Service (https://www.midwestls.com/Home)
> Provides acquisitions and cataloging services; cataloging records are provided only for items purchased through Midwest.

OCLC Connexion (https://help.oclc.org/Metadata_Services/Connexion)
> The member library interface for WorldCat, which allows members to download and edit bibliographic and authority records. A subscription to WorldCat provides access to over 450 million bibliographic records in nearly 500 languages, representing almost three billion physical and digital library resources.

SkyRiver (https://www.iii.com/products/skyriver/)
> Innovative Interfaces, Inc.'s database of bibliographic and authority records.

Titlewave (www.titlewave.com/)
> The resource ordering arm of Follett. Users of Follett Destiny can import MARC records for books purchased through Titlewave.

CATALOG MAINTENANCE AND AUTHORITY RECORD PROCESSING

ILS systems usually have some components or services that will assist with correcting catalog entries, including name, title, and subject access points. Some ILS systems feature automatic authority processing that utilizes authority records to update and correct bibliographic records. Some libraries choose to hire an authority vendor to oversee this function.

Backstage Library Works (https://www.bslw.com/.)
> A cataloging and authority vendor; services include automated authorities processing, digitization, and cataloging records.

MarcEdit (https://marcedit.reeset.net/)
> Free software for creating and editing bibliographic and authority MARC records from a variety of sources and in various languages.

MARCIVE (https://home.marcive.com/)
> This cataloging and authority vendor also provides automated authorities processing, database cleanup, and cataloging records, as well as automated delivery of government document records.

SUBSCRIPTION PRODUCTS

Cataloger's Desktop (www.loc.gov/cds/desktop/)
> Provides cataloging documentation, best practices, discussion list archives, manuals, and similar resources. While much of the content is available elsewhere, often free of charge, this resource brings much of it into one place and makes it easier to access.

Classification Web (https://classificationweb.net/)
Database of LC classification numbers and subject headings. Most helpful for those who need LC classification numbers. Subject headings are available through the LC Authorities website free of charge.

RDA Toolkit (http://access.rdatoolkit.org/)
Online version of the current cataloging rules via subscription.

Sears List of Subject Headings (https://searslistofsubjectheadings.com/subscription)
Used mostly by school and small public libraries. Please note that Sears subject headings have no relation to the CYAC headings and the lists are not interchangeable.

WebDewey (https://www.oclc.org/en/dewey/webdewey.html)
Online version of Dewey. Available for both full and abridged Dewey.

PRINT VERSIONS OF CATALOGING RESOURCES

Bristow, B. A., ed. *Sears List of Subject Headings*, 22nd ed. New York: H. W. Wilson, 2018.
Used mostly by school and small public libraries. Please note that Sears subject headings have no relation to the CYAC headings and the lists are not interchangeable. See subscription information to the print and online version at https://searslistofsubjectheadings.com/subscription.

Calimano, Iván E., and Ageo García, eds. *Sears: Lista de Encabezamientos de Materia: Nueva Traducción y Adaptación de la Lista Sears*. New York: H. W. Wilson, 2008.
Spanish-language adaptation of the Sears English-language list.

Cutter, C. A. *Cutter-Sanborn Three-Figure Author Table*. Chicopee, MA: H. R. Huntting Co. 1969.
The original Cutter tables have been expanded over the years by different people and are mutually incompatible. If the local library receives shelf-ready materials or purchases cataloging records with full call numbers, the library must be sure that the Cutter numbers are being provided from the same tables that the library uses.

Library of Congress Subject Headings
The full current headings are only available online at the LC Authorities website at https://authorities.loc.gov/. Additional subject cataloging resources, including links to PDF documents are available at https://www.loc.gov/aba/cataloging/subject/.

Mitchell, J. S., ed. *Abridged Dewey Decimal Classification and Relative Index*, 15th ed. Albany, NY: Forest Press, 2012.

Mitchell, J. S., ed. *Dewey Decimal Classification and Relative Index*, 23rd ed. Albany, NY: Forest Press, 2011. 4 vol.
Print-on-Demand copies are available at https://www.oclc.org/en/dewey/ordering.html.

ONLINE CATALOGING DISCUSSION LISTS

Many library associations host discussion lists that may or may not be specifically focused on cataloging topics. These may or may not require a person to be an association member to join the list.

Librarians should become aware of discussion lists related to their work, such as available through state library or school library associations. While there may not be a cataloging-specific list, there might be one that is generally useful, or that has a presence on social media. These may also be discovered by contacting the individual associations, which also might be willing to start new discussion lists.

AUTOCAT (https://listserv.syr.edu/scripts/wa.exe?A0=AUTOCAT)
This is a general discussion list used by authorities-work and cataloging staff in many types of libraries. Free to join, this discussion list is primarily used for questions and problems encountered by catalogers, although it occasionally includes discussions of broader interest.

LM_Net (www.lm-net.info/)
A general discussion list for school librarians (Library Media), which sometimes includes cataloging issues.

OLAC-L (https://olacinc.org/olac-l)
A discussion list hosted by the Online Audiovisual Catalogers group, but freely available to nonmembers. Questions and discussions focus on challenges arising in the cataloging of all kinds of nonbook materials.

RDA-L (https://lists.ala.org/sympa/info/rda-l)
Discussions are specifically related to the use of the RDA standard for descriptive cataloging and related topics and questions.

CATALOGING TEXTBOOKS AND OTHER SOURCES OF INFORMATION ON CATALOGING

Cataloging Calculator (http://calculate.alptown.com/)
Searchable database of Cutters and codes used in cataloging description, subject analysis, and classification. Also contains access to LCSH and LCC but does not include Dewey products or use.

Chan, Lois Mai, and Athena Salaba. *Cataloging and Classification: An Introduction,* 4th ed. Lanham, MD: Rowman and Littlefield, 2015.
A standard cataloging textbook.

Fountain, Joanna F. *Subject Headings for School and Public Libraries*, bilingual fourth ed. Santa Barbara, CA: Libraries Unlimited, 2012.
Authorized Library of Congress headings, with references and indexes in English and Spanish.

Haynes, Elizabeth, Joanna F. Fountain, and Michele Zwierski. *Unlocking the Mysteries of Cataloging: A Workbook of Examples*, 2nd ed. Santa Barbara, CA: Libraries Unlimited, 2015.
Illustrated exercises that focus on problems arising when cataloging books and other materials.

Intner, Sheila S., and Jean Weihs. *Standard Cataloging for School and Public Libraries*, 5th ed. Santa Barbara, CA: Libraries Unlimited, 2014.
A standard cataloging textbook.

Library of Congress. Network Development and MARC Standards Office. *MARC 21 Concise Format for Bibliographic Data*. 2004. www.loc.gov/marc/bibliographic/ecbdhome.html.
Gives information about all MARC fields with examples.

OCLC Bibliographic Formats and Standard (www.oclc.org/bibformats)
Gives information about all MARC fields with examples as implemented by OCLC. Also contains Connexion-specific documentation.

Principles of the Sears List of Subject Headings. Grey House Publishing, 2018.
A free resource that explains general principles of subject analysis and specifically how the *List* is applied. See https://searslistofsubjectheadings.com/page/principles.

Reitz, Joan M. *ODLIS—Online Dictionary for Library and Information Science. 2004-2014.;* www.abc-clio.com/ODLIS/odlis_A.aspx.
  A comprehensive dictionary of terminology related to library and information science or that might be encountered by librarians in the course of their work.

Satija, Mohinder Partap, and Elizabeth Haynes. *User's Guide to Sears List of Subject Headings*. Lanham, MD: Rowman and Littlefield, 2020.
  A guide to learning and applying headings from the *Sears List*.

Weihs, Jean, and Sheila S. Intner. *Beginning Cataloging*. Santa Barbara, CA: Libraries Unlimited, 2016.
  A standard cataloging textbook. https://products.abc-clio.com/ABC-CLIO Corporate/product.aspx?pc=A4790P.

WorldCat (www.worldcat.org)
  The public interface of OCLC, which can be used to find bibliographic information about an item; records can be viewed and copied manually but cannot be downloaded from this interface.

Z39.50 (www.loc.gov/z3950/)
  A protocol that allows users to download bibliographic records from other libraries that have set up the protocol, including the Library of Congress.

GLOSSARY

JOANNA F. FOUNTAIN

Bibliotechnics—Professional Library Services

AACR2 [*initialism*]. *Anglo-American Cataloguing Rules, 2nd edition*, the last edition of the international cataloging rules prior to the implementation of RDA. Available at https://www.alastore.ala.org/content/anglo-american -cataloguing-rules-second-edition-2002-revision-2005-update-kit. *See also* RDA.

Acronym. A series of initials that is pronounced as a word, such as MARC, or BISAC. Although acronyms usually stand for words, they may also stand alone, with no further meaning. *See also* Initialism.

Added access point. Any authorized entry provided as an access point beyond the primary access point in order to facilitate catalog searching of a name, title, or subject term. *See also* added entry; main entry; primary access point.

Added entry. An authorized heading other than the main entry (primary access point) provided as an added access point for catalog searching of any name, subject term, or title.

Analytical title. The title of a work contained in a more inclusive work (also called "an analytic"), which is not the same as the title proper of the inclusive work. An analytic is provided in a catalog record as an added access point, that is, the title of a part or section of a work, a chapter title, or any other title within the larger work being described.

Anime [*pronounced "ANN-ih-may"*]. Animated nonprint resources (television, film, video, etc.) that are easily identified by the style of colorful, stylized fantastic artwork of Japanese manga. Anime stories are often adult-themed, humorous, and characterized by characters drawn in with manga-style features such as large eyes and pointed chins, for example *Gabriel Dropout* from Doga Kobo. *See also* manga.

Authority records. Online records that establish the authorized form of entry for a name, preferred title, place, or topic, which enable catalog searches that yield all instances of that name, title, or topic regardless of the form found in a given source. While earlier card and printed files were created and used locally, the Library of Congress's authority file is available to the public on the web and in downloadable MARC format for any English-language catalog.

Authorized terms. Names of persons, places, topics, or works (titles) that have been designated as the terms that will be used within a given catalog or file. Such terms replace synonyms, alternate spellings, and related terms in order to gather results and increase searching efficiency.

BIBFRAME (**Bib**liographic **Frame**work). A Library of Congress-led project to build a replacement for the MARC encoding scheme, which is a more library-specific format. BIBFRAME is intended for use in libraries, archives, and museums by organizing information into three core levels of abstraction: *work*, *instance*, and *item*, using linked-data principles to increase access and use of bibliographic (cataloging) data within and beyond the library community (https://www.loc.gov/bibframe/). *See also* linked data; Library of Congress Authorities; MARC.

Bibliographic. Relating to books, other media, or listings or files of them. *See also* OCLC BibFormat.

Bibliographic identities. Names for persons or groups who use alternate identities, such as one or more pseudonyms, to identify their relationship to differing bibliographic resources. An example would be the author Isaac Asimov, one person, who wrote under his given name, Asimov, Isaac, 1920-1992, but also used two pseudonyms: French, Paul, 1920-1992, and Dr. "A", 1920-1992. Each name is a separate bibliographic identity. Such variant names for one person serve as useful references in a catalog, such as when there are resources related to one entity but identified by more than one, or a different name (https://www.loc.gov/catdir/cpso/pseud.pdf).

Bibliographic records. Cataloging records of books and other media created since the mid- to late 1900s, primarily in exchangeable electronic form (MARC). *See also* holdings records; item records.

Bibliographic utilities. Large databases that contain bibliographic data contributed by many sources, which are made available online, usually as part of a fee-based membership or subscription.

bidex [*acronym: pronounced "BUY-dex"; all lowercase*]. Source code for **Bilindex**, a bilingual Spanish-English subject heading list. Used in subfield 2 of 6xx fields with indicator values #7, for example, 650 #7 $aPadres y adolescentes. $2bidex. (See http://bilindex.com/.)

Bilingual. A person or resource that consistently uses two languages, either alternately or separately. Resources that are bilingual or multilingual (employing more than two languages) may be grouped by the least-used language in a library or classified normally by topic or form, with single-language (monolingual) materials.

BISAC [*acronym*]. **B**ook **I**ndustry **S**tandards **a**nd **C**ommunications, which produces the *BISAC Subject Heading List*, a hierarchical system of topical terms used primarily in categorizing items for sale in bookstores and online. *See also* bisacsh.

bisacsh [*acronym + "s-h," all lower case*]. Source code for the *Book Industry Standards and Communications Subject Headings* list. Used in subfield 2 of 6xx fields with indicator values #7, for example, 650 #7 $aJuvenile fiction. $2bisacsh. (See https://bisg.org/page/bisacedition.) *See also* BISAC.

Blu-ray. A high-capacity digital storage disc format capable of storing several hours of high-definition video. It is named for the blue-violet color of the laser used to read the data, which is stored at higher density than the red laser used to read DVDs. Because the discs look alike, one must read the disc label to determine whether it is a Blu-ray or DVD. Note that Blu-ray data cannot be read or played on a DVD player unless it is a modified or combination player. *See also* DVD; videorecording.

Book. The most common physical form of a textual work; also known as a printed monograph, volume, tome, or issue, depending on the context.

Call number. The location identifier leading to the physical location of an item in a library. Call numbers consist of one or more elements, such as numbers and letters, and any volume and copy numbers. It also refers to the label affixed to an item that allows it to be shelved or filed for retrieval.

Carrier. The physical medium, such as a tape or disc, in which data, sound, images, etc. are stored, sometimes in a housing (e.g., a cassette or cartridge) that is an integral part of the resource.

Cataloger's Desktop. A web-based subscription service that provides an integrated online documentation system containing or linking to more than a hundred key cataloging and metadata resources. Many are also freely available from the Library of Congress, such as the subject cataloging and MARC 21 manuals.

Cataloging. In library and information science, the practice and art of creating records and listings that include standardized physical descriptions, names and subject access terms, and location information for books and other media. Twenty-first century records (metadata) are most often electronic, while many older library catalogs worldwide are available only in card or print form.

CD [*initialism*]. **Compact Disc.** A digital optical disc containing machine-readable data. Developed for sound recordings, it is now used for storage of other types of computer data. *See also* CD-ROM; DVD.

CD-ROM [*pronounced "C, D, rahm"*]. **Compact Disc with Read-Only Memory.** A compact disc containing optical storage of text and/or audio and visual content, designed to be read or played on a computer, a dedicated player, or connected to a television. A CD-ROM cannot be changed, added to, or have content deleted. When spelled with a "k," the alternate spelling "disk" is normally reserved for magnetic storage of computer data, known more simply as a computer disk. *See also* CD; DVD.

CIP [*initialism: pronounced "C-I-P" or as the word "sip"*]. **C**ataloging-**i**n-**P**ublication is draft bibliographic data created primarily at the Library of Congress as a service to publishers and libraries. CIP is a block of data for catalog records created in advance of publication for titles that are most likely to be widely acquired by U.S. libraries. CIP is based on manuscript and other data, and usually printed on the verso of a book's title page. Catalogers must verify CIP data against the final product and add the missing data: the dimensions (actual measurements) and extent of the item (page counts, etc.), and a local call number. The local MARC record must also be corrected if the published work is different from the CIP data, for example, the title or the order of authors in the printed book.

Classification system. In cataloging, a systematic plan for arranging items according to a numerical or alphabetical system or code (notation) that represents a hierarchy of knowledge, designates the form of an item, and reflects significant facets of its contents. Dewey (the DDC) is the major system worldwide, whereas large libraries in some countries use the LCC scheme.

Coding (MARC). The activity or result of the activity involved in assigning numbers or letters (codes) to each element in a computer-readable bibliographic record. Such coding serves as instructions to the ILS or separate catalog program on a receiving computer, allowing it to parse the elements for display and searching in all types of collections.

Consortium. Membership collaboratives of one or more types of libraries, usually in a designated geographic area, that serve users indirectly through shared cataloging, interlibrary loan agreements, joint application for funding, and other means.

Continuing resources. Print or digital publications, usually with a single title, that are intended to be published indefinitely; issues usually carry numbers and/or dates. Types of continuing resources include serials, such as *National Geographic* magazine, and integrating resources, such as *Consumer Reports Online*. In MARC, cataloging records contain coded data in field 008, indicating whether the continuing resource is a serial component part (code b), an integrating resource (code i), or a serial (code s). *See also* resource.

Control field (MARC). One of several fields that contain alphanumeric codes that mark the beginning and end of each record's many elements, and which control the computer processing of bibliographic records formatted according to MARC standards. *See also* fixed field (MARC).

Copy cataloging. A cataloging activity short of "original" cataloging in which existing "copy" (bibliographic records) are adapted for local use. The most frequent sources of copy-cataloging records are the Library of Congress (https://catalog.loc.gov/) and various bibliographic utilities' websites. Some examples in this book are taken from the LC catalog. The local cataloger verifies the various data elements, and local data such as the call number or location code is added or changed as needed.

CRC [*initialism*]. A curriculum resource center, also known as an education collection, instructional resource center, learning resource center, or educational resource center, that houses a separate collection of materials in an academic library. CRCs support teacher education, classroom teaching, and parental cooperation as well as other types of work with children.

Cross reference. A short note at one place in a work or file that refers a reader to related information elsewhere in the same work or file. In library catalogs, these are also known as "see" or "see also" references. See also See reference; *See also* reference; reference.

CSH [*initialism*]. *The Children's Subject Headings List* is a list of terms devised and maintained by LC's Children's and Young Adult staff, who tailor "main" LCSH terms to the needs and reading levels of children and young adults, especially in school and public library catalogs. CSH terms are included in both CIP and online cataloging records (https://www.loc.gov/aba/cyac/childsubjhead.html).

Cutter number, or **Cutter.** A series of numbers assigned to each letter of the alphabet. A number represents a filing name or word and is used for ease of shelving or filing as a decimal number. In larger collections, the number is usually followed by a title "workmark," or letter, for further sequencing of multiple resources by a given author, for example, T649h for Tolkien's *The Hobbit*. *See also* workmark.

Cutter, or **Cutter-Sanborn table.** A table devised by Charles Ammi Cutter in which the initial letter of an entry (usually the surname of the first author) is matched with a series of numbers based on English-language frequency. The numbers are used for arranging items alphabetically within each classification, for example, T649 for "Tolkien." The same number is used whether the work is by or about the person, then the workmark reflects its role: the workmark for a work is the filing/first word of the title; for biographies, it is the first letter of the author's surname. Copies of printed editions and Cutter-generating sites are available online; printed tables provide for either two or three digits ("figures"), which may also be generated online at www.unforbi.com.ar/cutteren/. OCLC's four-digit generator may be accessed at https://help.oclc.org/Metadata_Services/WebDewey/Dewey_Cutter_Program. However, it is very important for each library to use the numbers from *only one edition or version* in order to prevent conflicts, as each uses different numbers.

CYAC [*pronounced "kayak"*]. The **C**hildren's and **Y**oung **A**dults' **C**ataloging Program (a part of the Literature Section at the Library of Congress) adjusts subject headings to plain language and creates draft CIP records primarily to benefit children and youth using school and public libraries (https://www.loc.gov/aba/cyac/index.html).

DCM [*initialism*]. The Library of Congress's *Descriptive Cataloging Manual* is updated periodically online and in PDF format by LC's Standards and Policy Division (https://www.loc.gov/aba/publications/FreeDCM/freedcm.html).

Delimiter (MARC). A character or symbol (e.g., $, ≠, |, or _) used in front of each subfield letter in a MARC record that tells a computer that a different piece of information follows it. *See also* subfield (in MARC).

Dewey Decimal Classification, or **DDC.** The **D**ewey **D**ecimal **C**lassification is a numeric system for identifying aspects of the subject or subjects treated in published works and providing numbers and labels for items to be shelved digit-by-digit, or decimally. The most widely used classification system, consisting of full, abridged, and translated editions, now developed at the Library of Congress and made available by print-on-demand and online, and in OCLC's WebDewey product. Structured in ten hierarchically subdivided classes (classification groups), the system maintains the relative subject relationship of one resource to another. Examples include works about animal husbandry (636) arranged by type of animal, and geographical works (910) sub-arranged regionally and locally. Free DDC summaries (the "Dewey Tens") are available from OCLC at https://www.oclc.org/content/dam/oclc/dewey/resources/summaries/deweysummaries.pdf. *See also* WebDewey.

Display constant. A value in a record that causes information to be displayed to users in a different and more meaningful way than is entered directly in the record; the displayed version is usually system-generated, and is based on the coding of a variable field in a record. For example, in a Target Audience Note field coded "521 0# $a 2.3," the first indicator value of "0" generates the display constant "Reading grade level," while "2.3" represents the third month of the second grade, the estimated reading level for the resource.

Dublin Core. The Dublin Core Schema began as a small set of fifteen vocabulary terms used to describe digital resources and physical resources. The name reflects the Ohio city where the schema originated in 1995. The schema has been expanded and is now maintained by the Dublin Core Metadata Initiative (DCMI), a not-for-profit membership organization that supports innovation in metadata (https://www.dublincore .org/specifications/dublin-core/dcmi-terms/).

DVD [*initialism*]. A digital video disc, usually compact (4¾ in.) that contains visual content, such as a movie, which is frequently accompanied by sound and some text and electronic content, such as captioning software. Some DVDs have captioning in languages beyond that of the sound track, and may include closed captioning for hearing-impaired persons, or audio description for listeners who are visually impaired. A DVD may be played or read on a computer and/or some players or televisions but may not be changed in any way. *See also* CD; CD-ROM; Blu-ray.

Facet. Any identifiable or definable aspect of a subject or an object; in cataloging, a term that qualifies or limits a broader concept or broader content.

FAST [*acronym*]. The Faceted Application of Subject Terminology project provides an authorized subject list that includes terms derived from LCSH (https:// www.oclc.org/research/themes/data-science/fast.html). Its searchFAST interface serves as an index to WorldCat, and is designed to help users understand, control, apply and use terms in that database, and to convert LCSH terms to FAST headings when necessary. For example, a search for the FAST term "Recipe books" leads to records using the subject term "Cookbooks," which is authorized for LCSH as well as for the FAST list.

Field (MARC). A numbered line or paragraph in a bibliographic record, usually numbered in MARC templates, and which includes at least one subfield. When the first subfield is "$a," those two characters are implied, and may be omitted from the local record's MARC display.

Field tag (MARC). The number at the beginning of a MARC field indicating the nature of its content. For example, the 245 field contains the title and statement of responsibility that appear in designated places on a resource. *See also* tag.

Fixed field (MARC). A leading field of several brief, fixed-length letters and numbers that tell a computer how to process a record. Also known as the "control" field, the fixed field is found at the beginning of most MARC templates. *See also* control field.

FRBR [*pronounced "FER-ber"*]. The "Functional Requirements of Bibliographic Records" comprise a conceptual entity-relationship model developed by members of IFLA as a way of associating resources with works in varying manifestations and iterations, such as an individual copy of a given recording of an operatic interpretation of a literary work. *See also* WEMI.

Genre heading. A term similar to a subject heading, but which reflects what a resource is (its actual form) rather than what the resource is about. When a term is authorized for use in both cases, its intended meaning is reflected in field tag 655 for the resource's form. Tag 650 reflects the subject matter of the resource. For example, for a resource that is an atlas: (a compilation of maps) 655 #0 $a Maps. By contrast, a resource that is about maps (cartography in general) would have this subject entry: 650 #0 $a Maps. Similar examples using the same term for either genre or subject matter are: Feature films, Video recordings for the hearing impaired, Jazz, Children's films, and Musicals. To determine the authorized usage of any given term, search the authority file for the term under Subject, then note the "Type of Heading" in the right-hand column for each authorized term (https://authorities.loc.gov/). *See also* gmgpc; lcgft; lcshac; Library of Congress Authorities.

Genre subdivisions. A cataloger may provide access to a resource using a combination of subject terms to describe both its content *and* its form or genre. A genre or form subdivision may be added in subfield "v" after a subject term, thus narrowing the meaning of the term in subfield "a." Many such terms may be used also as main subject terms, as when the resource is about a genre. There are special usage exceptions for terms describing juvenile materials. These may be found, with instructions, at https://www.loc.gov/aba/publications/FreeLCSH/LCSH41%20CSH%20 intro.pdf, page CSH-ii. For example, a fictional juvenile book about dinosaurs, found in a library also used by adults, would have the topical term "Dinosaurs" in subfield "a," and a "v" subfield: 650 #0 $aDinosaurs $v Juvenile fiction. The equivalent entry for the same book, found in a library used primarily by children, would be 650 #1 $aDinosaurs $vFiction. Note that the second indicator is "1" and that "Juvenile" subdivisions are not used in children's library catalogs. *See also* genre heading.

GMD [*initialism*]. General material designation is one of a number of broad category designators for the many formats of nonbook material. The GMD was introduced in *AACR2* for ready identification of nonbook formats and is still found in square brackets in MARC field 245 subfield "h" [immediately following the title in subfield "a"] in some catalogs that incorporate RDA practices. For example, "[videorecording]" is a general designation (GMD) authorized in AACR2, whereas "videodisc" is a designation for a specific format (SMD), which was authorized within the broader category and used in the 300 field. Note, however, that while some earlier GMD terms are mapped in RDA to Content Type in field 336, neither GMDs nor SMDs are used as such in RDA practice. *See also* SMD.

gmgpc [*initialism; all lower case*]. Source code for the *Thesaurus for Graphic Materials II: Genre & Physical Characteristic Terms (TGM II)*, compiled by the Prints and Photographs Division of the Library of Congress (https://www.loc.gov/rr/print/tgm2/). Terms are applied primarily to archival materials; they are used in subfield 2 of field 655 with indicator values #7, for example, 655 #7 $aGroup portraits. $2gmgpc. *See also* lcgft.

Graphic novels. Print resources that consist of comic-book-style drawings telling a story or informing through graphic depiction, and frequently directed at a youthful audience. In common usage, the term is used to include nonfiction as well as fictional works. Examples include *New Kid* by Jerry Craft [fiction], *Around the World* by Matt Phelan [nonfiction], and some illustrated classics. While nonfictional graphical works would normally be classified topically, libraries sometimes group them by format along with other graphical works, as when the library has few such titles. Some are drawn using a black-and-white art style called manga, a Japanese term for comic books. Other terms for graphical works include comic books, fotonovelas, cartoons, caricatures, and comic strips. *See also* manga.

gsafd [*initialism; all lower case*]. Source code for an early list of genre and form headings, *Guidelines on Subject Access to Individual Works of Fiction, Drama, Etc.* Applies to works of literature and describes what a work is rather than what it is about. It is used in subfield 2 of field 655 with indicator values #7; for example, 655 #7 $aAdventure fiction. $2gsafd.

Holdings records. Holdings records contain the specific information about resources that are held or owned by a given library or group of libraries: their location(s), which specific items are held (e.g., parts of a resource), their publication patterns (e.g., frequency of issue), and related notes. This type of record depends on and is linked to the related bibliographic records. The data in the 8xx fields is formatted for easy identification of particular parts or items held. An example for one issue of a periodical might be "v.3: no.2 (2019: Autumn)." *See also* bibliographic records; item records.

IBBY [*acronym*]. The International Board on Books for Young People is a network of people who connect children and youth with books that promote international understanding and good will; based in Switzerland.

IFLA [*acronym: pronounced "IF-lah"*]. The International Federation of Library Associations and Institutions, an international body based in The Hague, was founded to promote universal and equitable access to information, ideas, and works through libraries, other information professional organizations, and UNESCO (https://www.ifla.org/). International standards developed by IFLA inform, and are the basis for, RDA, the most recent standard for describing library resources in the online environment.

ILS [*initialism*]. An integrated library system is a library system consisting of a series of interactive online modules serving a variety of functions, such as ordering, processing and tracking, cataloging, searching, circulation, and status information of items related to one or more libraries.

Index. A print or electronic list of terms, usually alphabetized, created to facilitate finding information in a printed or electronic book, document, file, or the internet. A numerical index provides comparisons that show the value of something by comparing it to something else whose value is known.

Indicators (MARC). Two single-digit positions that follow tags 1xx-9xx in the MARC record, defining (indicating) how a computer should treat the content; these eye-readable characters also help a person interpret the content of the field. When an indicator position is undefined, that condition is represented by a "blank" character, sometimes indicated by the # ("pound" or "number") character.

Initialism. A series of initials that are pronounced individually (rather than as a word), such as ISBN or LC. *See also* Acronym.

ISBN [*initialism: pronounced "I-S-B-N" or "IZ-bin"*]. International Standard Book Numbers are individual nation-specific ten- or thirteen-digit numbers that are also used on nonprint resources. ISBNs are uniquely assigned to each separate edition and variation (except reprintings) of a publication; based on the earlier SBN (Standard Book Numbering) format. Official ISBNs for purchase and use in new U.S. publications are available only from Bowker (www.bowker.com/products/ISBN-US.html). *See also* ISSN.

ISSN [*initialism*]. International Standard Serial Numbers are individual eight-digit numbers that identify such continuing publications as magazines and newspapers—some of which are nonprint resources. The electronic e-ISSN for a serial is different from the ISSN for the print version of the same serial. All ISSNs are linked by an ISSN-L to the number for the first published medium. ISSNs for serials published in the United States are assigned only by the U.S. ISSN Center at LC (https://www.loc.gov/issn/). *See also* ISBN.

Item records. Item records are attached to individual bibliographic (catalog) records for each physical item held by the library. They describe what type of resource the item is, its physical aspects, and its location (including call number) and internal barcode number. This data allows for specific items to be tracked for circulation or for movement within the system. There may be multiple item records attached to a specific holdings record for a given bibliographic record, as one must be created and maintained for each individually circulating item, even when it is just part of a given resource. For example, an item record could be created for one, some, or all the contents of a box containing two or more items that may circulate or move individually. *See also* bibliographic records; holdings records.

LC [*initialism*]. The Library of Congress supports the U. S. Congress and functions as a national library via its online catalog and other services. All LC publications are in the public domain within the United States.

LC Linked Data Service. The Linked Data Service enables both humans and machines to programmatically access authority data at the Library of Congress. This service is influenced by—and implements—the Linked Data movement's approach of exposing and interconnecting data on the web.

LCC [*initialism*]. The *Library of Congress Classification* system is based on letters of the English alphabet and is followed by positive whole numbers. It divides subjects into broad categories and provides a guide to the books in the Library of Congress's collections. While the LCC system was designed specifically for the LC's own collections, many other large libraries (especially academic libraries) use it to organize their own collections.

LCCN [*initialism*]. The Library of Congress Control Number is an individual number automatically assigned sequentially as each additional resource is cataloged [four-digit date + six-digit sequence number]. This number may be found in the CIP data and used to search the LC catalog (https:// catalog.loc.gov/). For example, 2006019518 leads to *The End* by Lemony Snicket.

lcgft [*initialism; all lower case*]. Source code for the Library of Congress Genre/ Form Terms for Library and Archival Materials list. It is used to describe what a work is, rather than what it is about, such as a work about themes or topics in current "Children's films" (subject, in field 650) versus an actual film or videorecording produced especially for children (form). Used in subfield 2 of field 655 with indicator values #7, for example, 655 #7 $a Children's films. $2lcgft. *See also* gsafd; gmgpc.

LCNAF [*initialism*]. Library of Congress Name Authority File, an online database of records containing the authorized forms of personal names, corporate bodies, geographic and other jurisdictions, preferred titles, named meetings, etc.; these records include related and unused names and source information.

LCSH [*initialism*]. *Library of Congress Subject Headings* is the subject heading list accepted worldwide as the English-language standard; originally issued in print as "the big red books," authority records for its use are now freely available online. Due to its use in records supplied by vendors and free availability online, LCSH, including CYAC usage, is increasingly used instead of Sears headings in school library catalogs.

lcsh [*initialism; all lower case*]. Source code for the *Library of Congress Subject Headings,* used for terms used in subfield 2 of 6xx fields with indicator values #7, for example, 650 #7 $aAdventure stories. $2lcsh. Most English-language records use 6xx fields with #0 indicator values to designate LCSH terms. *See also* CSH; lcshac.

lcshac [*initialism; all lower case*]. Source code for *Children's Subject Headings* (CSH) in *Library of Congress Subject Headings: Supplementary Vocabularies*, a list of substitute terms commonly used in catalogs used by children and youth and adults working with them. The code is used in subfield 2 of 6xx fields with indicator value #1, for example, 650 #1 $aBabies. $2lcshac. *See also* CSH; lcsh.

lcsh-es [*initialism; all lower case*]. Source code for the bilingual website *Library of Congress Subject Headings in Spanish* is *Encabezamientos de materia LC en español* (https://lcsh-es.org), which lists several Spanish-language translations of LCSH terms from various sources, with no one source preferred. The code is used in subfield 2 of 6xx fields with indicator values #7, for example, 650 #7 $aCuentos escolares. $2lcsh-es.

Library catalog. A file or list representing the holdings or accessible titles of one or more libraries, generally online, but also in stand-alone computers and older card catalogs or printed lists.

Library of Congress Authorities. A public online file of headings continuously established and authorized by the Library of Congress as a controlled vocabulary, with new terms being added and others updated regularly. This database of authority records is used daily throughout the world by libraries and organizations for browsing and viewing authorized headings for subjects, names, titles, and genres. These records, which are in MARC format, may be accessed directly at https://authorities.loc.gov/ for viewing or for downloading into library catalogs. *See also* lcsh; lcshac; lcgft.

Linked data. Data published in accordance with principles designed to facilitate linkages among datasets, element sets, and value libraries. This type of data enables humans and machines to programmatically access interconnected data on the web. *See also* BIBFRAME.

LMS [*initialism*]. An LMS, or Library Management System, incorporates features that make it possible for libraries to keep track of a library's collections while providing searchers with efficient access to those resources. *See also* ILS; LSP.

LSP [*initialism*]. An LSP, or Library Services Platform, is an advanced, "next generation" LMS that is designed to add features to an ILS. For example, it would provide access to online cloud services and web technologies, and aid in managing physical, digital and electronic materials in a unified system. *See also* ILS; LMS.

Main entry. The primary access point in a cataloging record, most often the authorized form of the name of the first or only creator (personal or corporate) of a work; also, the basis for the alphabetizing element in a call number. When the main entry in a MARC record is a name, it is always given in a "1xx" field. All other names, titles, and name/title combinations in a record may be included as added access points (added entries) for identifying a resource. *See also* primary access point; added access point; added entry.

Manga [*pronounced "MANG-guh"*]. Graphic works frequently published as series or periodicals that normally follow one plot across multiple comparatively short issues or volumes, which may be intended for older youth or adult readers. Manga are usually read from right to left—even in English. Manga artwork is usually black and white, and quite different from art used in Western graphic novels, which are usually printed in color and intended for younger audiences. This style is also used in animated works known as anime, for example, *Kitaro's Strange Adventures* by Shigeru Mizuki. *See also* anime; graphic novels.

MARC [*acronym pronounced "mark"*]. **MA**chine **R**eadable **C**ataloging is the standard for formatting cataloging records for computer processing in multiple systems and platforms, but also eye-readable for cataloging purposes. *See also* MARC format; MARC 21 format; MARCXML format.

MARC format. A coding system created for the Library of Congress in the 1960s by Henriette Avram for describing and processing records for resources being cataloged at the Library. The use of the MARC format results in records that can be read by a person or a computer with appropriate software; they may also be shared among libraries electronically for use on standard platforms. Widely used since the early 1970s in various iterations; most international versions have been harmonized as MARC 21. *See also* BIBFRAME.

MARC 21 format [*acronym, pronounced "mark twenty-one"*]. Updated format standard issued by the Library of Congress in 1999 that is currently in use; it incorporates new technologies as well as protocols from the international library community. This format is maintained by LC and is used in many countries for electronic records containing bibliographic, authority, holdings, classification, and community data.

MARCXML format [*acronym + initials, pronounced "mark X-M-L"*]. An aggregation format that is easy for various systems to parse; developed and used by the Library of Congress and others to facilitate sharing and networked access to bibliographic information.

MARCXML toolkit, or **MARC 21 Schema.** A set of conversion tools available at the LC website that allow full character set conversion to and from files in both MARC format and other formats (https://www.loc.gov/standards/marcxml/).

Metadata. Data that provides information about other data, including descriptive metadata such as cataloging records, which is used to discover and identify things. When books and other informational media are described, the data elements provide titles, names of responsible persons, and a variety of keywords that may be imbedded in abstracts or annotations.

mrc [*initialism, all lower case*]. The most common filename extension used to distinguish MARC records, or files, from other file types (e.g., .txt or other textual files) for seamless transfer from one computer to another.

Nonbook. A resource that is not a book—although it may be textual—such as a poster, microform, computer file, or printed music that may look like a book. The term also may refer pejoratively to a printed book that is of no real substance or merit.

Nonprint. A term sometimes used loosely to describe nonbook materials or media, such as electronic files and recorded media, but also such resources as maps, games, and posters, for which more accurate and specific terms should be used.

OCLC [*initialism*]. A nonprofit member organization established in Ohio in 1967 that serves primarily as a cooperative cataloging utility. It also hosts WorldCat, which provides for public access to the holdings of thousands of libraries worldwide and is the source for DDC resources. It was originally known as the Ohio College Library Center, later as the Online Computer Library Center, and now simply as OCLC, Inc.

OCLC BibFormat [*initialism + "Bib Format"*]. *Bibliographic Formats and Standards* is OCLC's guide to decoding and entering bibliographic information in the WorldCat database of MARC records. Also known as OCLCBib, it includes OCLC's tagging conventions and input standards, and provides many examples, freely available and frequently accessed by catalogers, including copy catalogers, instructors, and non-OCLC members, at https://www.oclc.org/bibformats/en/about.html. *See also* WorldCat.

OPAC [*pronounced "OH-pack"*]. Online Public Access Catalog, the electronic version of a library's catalog, set up especially for public use. Although it may be viewed in alphabetical order, an OPAC may be searched using various drop-down menu choices and further limited in various ways, such as relevance, date, and collection. An abbreviated call number search may present resources in an order that begin with a partial call number, but the results are not as comprehensive as those in a shelflist, in which staff may view all resources in shelving order, either numerical (Dewey) or alphabetical (LCC). An OPAC view does not provide the same level of detail as that found in a staff view. *See also* shelflist.

Open date. An open-ended date, followed by a hyphen, given in the MARC subfield for "Date of publication, distribution, etc." (fields 260 or 264, subfield "c") to denote the first date of issue for a continuing resource. Also used for the birth year of a person, or the beginning date of an ongoing event, and most often found in subfields containing subdivisions. Examples include 260 ## $c1923- [for *Time*, a current magazine]; 600 10 $aSofia Vergara, $d1972- [for the birth year of a person, as in a biography].

Outsourced cataloging. Bibliographic data services obtained from outside sources, usually purchased by a library on a fee basis, either from a resource vendor, a bibliographic utility, or a contractor. Such services may be part of the acquisitions process, or secured after resources have been received by purchase, gift, or other means. The term "outsourced" may refer to free or purchased services that partially or completely replace internal cataloging functions or services.

Parallel title. The part of a title that is found on the preferred source and is in a different language or script from the first title on the resource. Parallel titles proper are always preceded by an equal sign [=] in subfield "b" of field 245 of a MARC record, indicating that they are equal or alternative versions of the title proper. An example would be 245 10 $aBear takes a trip = $bL'ours fait un voyage. There may be more than one parallel title, as in the case of multilingual (versus bilingual) resources.

Preferred title. The version of a title that has been established (usually by the Library of Congress) as the authorized entry form for works that have appeared in more than one language, or for which there are versions with variants of the title. For example, "Cinderella," a story character who has appeared in many forms, languages, and iterations for hundreds of years, is also the preferred title for English-language catalogs. Previously known as uniform titles, the preferred titles of ancient works vary from language to language, with "Cenicienta" being used in Spanish-speaking countries, "Cendrillon" in French, and so on. The currently preferred English-language titles are available under "Title Authority Headings" and "Name/Title Authority Headings" at https://authorities.loc.gov. Preferred titles are used in MARC fields 130, 240, 630, 730, and 700 12 subfield "t" ($t).

Primary access point. The RDA term for the AACR2 term "Main entry," which is the authorized version of a name or title (main entry) in a MARC record. It functions as the basis for further entries, such as added names and alternate versions of the title of a resource, and to differentiate among resources with the same title. When the primary access point is a name (field 100), it is the name of the first or only creator (personal or corporate) of a work. When there is no creator given in a 1xx field, the default primary access point is the title of the resource as given in field 245, for example 245 00 $aFrozen, a motion picture resource for which there is no 1xx field. In other cases, the title in the 245 field may be transformed into a preferred title and entered in field 130. The primary access point is the basis for the alphabetizing element (Cutter number) in a call number. The same type of title may also appear in some other fields, such as 630 or especially 730, with functions defined for that field. All other names, titles, and name/title combinations in a record that are included are known as added access points (added entries) for identifying a resource. The authorized forms of names, preferred titles, etc. can be verified at https://authorities.loc.gov/. *See also* main entry.

Public services. Activities that take place in the public areas of a library, as distinguished from other areas. Such activities include circulation, reference services, shelving, instruction, public relations, and related activities. In smaller and low-staff libraries, these functions often overlap substantially with activities that might otherwise take place in less-public areas. *See also* technical services.

RDA [*initialism*]. **R**esource **D**escription and **A**ccess is the most recent international cataloging standard (issued in 2010, implemented in 2013), which is updated with subsequent revisions (as described at http://rda-rsc.org/content/about-rda). RDA replaces (and in some libraries supplements) AACR2. *See also* AACR2.

RDA Toolkit. A stand-alone collection of online and print RDA-related documents and resources, other policy and standards documents, LC's Cataloger's Desktop, and the RDA standard itself. Links to RDA Toolkit are available from a variety of products, including library systems. The online version is an integrated, browser-based product available only by paid subscription to those documents and resources. The full-text print version, *RDA: Resource Description and Access*, is available for purchase at https://www.rdatoolkit.org/rdaprint. *See also* RDA.

Recon. *See* retrospective conversion.

Reference. In text, catalogs, and similar resources, information that refers the reader to another passage within the same resource, or to a different resource. An online reference is often hyperlinked to that passage or resource for easy access. *See also* cross reference.

Reference work. A resource, such as a dictionary or encyclopedia, used for quick access to multiple items of information. Entries in such works are usually brief, often arranged alphabetically, written in an informative style, and are not intended to be read from beginning to end.

Resource. In RDA, a broad term used to refer to the wide scope of materials being acquired and cataloged in libraries today, such as books and other printed or nonprinted text items, non-text resources computer and online files, and unpublished resources. *See also* RDA; continuing resources.

Retrospective conversion. The activities involved in "recon," the processes involved in transitioning from a manual to an automated cataloging and catalog-management system, especially from a card catalog to an online catalog using records in MARC format. Most school and public libraries have made this change due to public demand and the availability of affordable and free options and complex automated systems.

Romanization. A system, or process of converting written or spoken text from a different writing system to the Roman (Latin) script, that is, the transliteration or transcription of characters and words into Roman script. The list Romanization tables recommended by ALA and LC is available at https://www.loc.gov/catdir/cpso/roman.html.

Sears. The *Sears List of Subject Headings* is a subject authority primarily used in schools and other small libraries as an alternative to LCSH; also available in Spanish. *See also* slem.

sears [*all lower case*]. Source code for terms from the *Sears List of Subject Headings*. Used in subfield 2 of 6xx fields with indicator values #7, for example, 650 #7 $aAbsentee parents. $2sears.

See reference. A short note in a work or file that refers the reader from an unused term to a different/correct entry where the information is located. In MARC-formatted authority files, for example, an entry in a 4xx field is a See reference, indicating that the entry being viewed is not the entry authorized for use in library catalogs. *See also* cross reference; reference; see also reference.

See also reference. A short note in a work or file that refers the reader to additional authorized entries and/or related information. In authority files, for example, an entry in a MARC-formatted 5xx field is a "See also" reference, indicating that the entry being viewed may be used as well as the entry given in the 1xx field, if either or both entries are needed; in such cases both terms would be authorized for appropriate application in library catalogs. *See also* cross reference; reference; see reference.

Segmentation mark. An informational slash (/) or prime (') used in the classification number in field 082 of a bibliographic record to indicate the end of the shortest suggested or correct DDC number for a given topic. This punctuation is used only in the online record; it is never used on item labels (call number labels) or in the holdings field of a cataloging record.

Series. A title assigned to related multiple items, often by one author, that may be bought or read separately, but that do not constitute a set that is bought as one title (e.g., encyclopedias).

Shared catalog. A library management system containing the records of more than one library (e.g., those of the members of a library consortium or system) that allows the exchange and sharing of records and resources, primarily through interlibrary loan services.

Shelflist. An internal (i.e., not public) catalog arranged in the order of items on a shelf or in a file. This type of file is maintained in a library's technical services area, and is arranged by classification and Cutter numbers, item by item, for internal use for inventory and recording decisions or internal notes about specific items. Although much of their function has been transferred to online systems, a library may maintain a card version of the shelflist, or a "frozen" version of it for historical or other information (e.g., donor names or price data) that is not included in its online or public catalogs. A few libraries continue to maintain shelflists in card format, either as a backup to an online system, or as an internal working file. In either case, a shelflist or online search by call number will yield information about numbers in local use for a given subject, person, or the like, as well as what is actually available in a particular classification within a library. When a library's cataloging policy requires unique call numbers, shelflisting functions help to determine these. *See also* OPAC; shelflisting.

Shelflisting. When adding a resource to a catalog, the prospective call number is checked in the online catalog to be sure that it is not an exact duplicate of one that has been assigned to another resource, and that it fits logically with other resources around it. It is important to do this in libraries that require unique call numbers for each resource or item, and to document policies that reflect local practice, such as this statement for one library (https://web.library.yale.edu/book/export/html/817). *See also* OPAC; shelflist.

shsples [*initialism; all lower case*]. Source code for the bilingual (English-Spanish) edition of *Subject Headings for School and Public Libraries*. Used in subfield 2 of 6xx fields with indicator values #7, for example, 650 #7 $aDía de los niños. $2shsples.

slem [*acronym; all lower case*]. Source code for the Spanish-language version of the *Sears* subject heading list: *Sears: lista de encabezamientos de materia*. Used in subfield 2 of 6xx fields with indicator values #7, for example, 650 #7 $aLiteratura española. $2slem.

SMD [*initialism*]. Specific Material Designation, a term used in AACR2 to describe any one of many narrow categories of physical objects and other nonbook materials, versus a general material designation [GMD]. For example, although now called "Carrier Type" in RDA, the narrower "SMD" term "videodisc" is used in MARC field 300, subfield "a," whereas the broader, general designation "[videorecording]" would have been used in subfield "h" of field 245 under AACR2 rules. Neither SMDs nor GMDs are used in RDA practice. Catalogs often supplement or replace this textual information with a variety of icons that identify carrier types visually. The current list of specific material form terms for field 300, subfield "a" is posted at https://www.loc.gov/standards/valuelist/marcsmd.html. *See also* GMD.

Standard numbers. Numbers of varying lengths, assigned from various standards, that publishers and producers use to designate each unique iteration of a resource, such as the item's ISBN, UPC, or music or video number. While standard numbers were originally assigned for point-of-sale inventory purposes, standard numbers are included in many bibliographic records, making them searchable in library catalogs. Librarians must, however, be alert to the occasional reuse of a given standard number, as publishers do not always apply new numbers on new iterations; incorrect numbers must be coded as such in order to prevent searching errors. *See also* ISBN; UPC.

Subfield (in MARC). A separately coded portion of each MARC field that contains content different from any other subfield in that field. Each letter or number code, such as "a," is preceded by a defining character called a delimiter such as a dollar mark ($), a pipe (|), or a double dagger (‡) that is used for interpreting the record's individual elements visually and is used by computers for accurate processing. *See also* delimiter (MARC).

Subject entry. A field or entry in a cataloging record, taken from a controlled vocabulary, that indicates that a described work is about a given topic, such as the authorized name of a person, place, or thing; or even the title of another work, such as a criticism of that work.

Subject heading. A term in a controlled vocabulary, designed for catalogs, bibliographies, and virtual libraries, that facilitates effective and targeted searching in a given language. For example, LCSH (the most extensive list of English-language subject headings) guides a cataloger or user from alternate terms for a given subject to a single authorized term, or heading, for that subject. For example, "Musical plays" leads to "Musicals," the preferred subject heading authorized for use in the authorized LCSH vocabulary.

Tag (MARC). A three-digit number that precedes and identifies each field in a MARC record. Tags *001-009* begin the sequence; the remaining tags, 010-999, are followed by two indicators and at least one coded subfield. When only subfield "a" is used, however, some systems assume, and therefore do not display the $a coding. *See also* field tag (MARC).

Tagging (MARC). The assignment of numbers to fields in MARC records.

Technical services. Activities that take place beyond the public areas of a library. Such activities include collection development, order processing, cataloging, system management, physical preparation for circulation, and audiovisual services. *See also* public services.

Thesaurus. A controlled set of terms from a particular area of knowledge (rather than knowledge in general), linked by hierarchical or associative relations and equivalence relations (synonyms) with natural language terms. An example is the *Thesaurus of ERIC Descriptors* for education-related research.

Title proper. The chief (main) title of a resource, including any alternative title, but excluding parallel titles and such other title information as subtitles. In MARC records, the title proper is entered in the first subfield ($a) of field 245 and is a requirement for saving or filing a record in a library system.

Uniform title. In earlier cataloging standards, this is the term for the version of a title established (usually by the Library of Congress) as the authorized entry. This form of a title is used in MARC fields 130, 240, 630 and 730, and titles in subfield "t" of field 700 12. These are known as "preferred" titles in RDA and are primarily used for works that have appeared in more than one language, or for which there are variant versions of a given title. *See also* preferred title.

Unmediated. An RDA term used to categorize a type of resource that requires no equipment or device for a person to access its content; a printed book or graphic resource, for example, is unmediated. The term "unmediated" (not capitalized) is used in subfield "a" of MARC field 337 to indicate the media type of the resource.

UPC [*initialism*]. A **U**niversal **P**roduct **C**ode is a unique international standard number designed for point-of-sale transactions. Often found immediately below an item's barcode, it can be read by a scanner or by the human eye. It is used in cataloging records for correctly identifying and searching a resource. Although the original UPC for an item may have a new code label placed over it, UPCs appear on all identical items from a given publisher, producer, or manufacturer, and represent the item's actual selling price and other characteristics. UPC codes are also searchable in most catalogs as Standard numbers, where they can help to distinguish editions and formats of works, such as various bindings of books and video recordings of the same title.

Variable field (MARC). A field in a MARC record that may vary in length and content. Variable fields are identified by three-digit numeric tags, which identify the nature of the content of each field.

Video recording. *See* Blu-ray; DVD.

Videorecording. *See* Blu-ray; DVD.

Virtual library. A digital collection of online resources for viewing and hearing, and with which a person may interact to various extents. Such resources are often e-books, audiobooks, music recordings, films, research data, or online learning materials, which may be accessed using a computer or mobile device.

WebDewey. An online database providing access to the Dewey Decimal Classification (DDC), and the Abridged Dewey Classification, hosted and maintained by OCLC. This paid-subscription database is a full representation of all published numbers, mappings, and new terms approved by the Dewey Editorial Policy Committee.

WEMI [*initialism: pronounced "W-E-M-I," or "WEH-mee"*]. A four-level philosophical and conceptual hierarchy that lets a cataloger identify a resource on up to four levels (**W**ork, **E**xpression, **M**anifestation, **I**tem) using the FRBR model, and allows a searcher to find one exemplar of one manifestation of an expression of a given work in a catalog or database. For examples, see https://web.library.yale.edu/cataloging/music/frbr-wemi-music.

Workform. A template designed for use in creating records that are uniform in content, sequence, and format for a given ILS. In cataloging, a template used to create original MARC records for subsequent loading into an electronic catalog.

Workmark. In libraries with collections using Dewey call numbers, one or more letters following a Cutter number (for an author or title) that represent the title or subject of a work. Examples include the letter "s" representing the word "Selected" in Robert Frost's "Selected Poems" = F76s, or the letter "b" in F76b for the author (Brown) of a biography of Robert Frost (the subject). In this example, "F76" is the Cutter number for Robert Frost.

WorldCat [*acronym*]. A database containing millions of cataloging records created and maintained by member libraries that participate in OCLC. It is freely available on the web at https://www.worldcat.org/ as an informational resource for identifying, locating, and viewing (but not downloading) bibliographic records for materials in contributing libraries nearby or around the world. *See also* OCLC BibFormat.

Z39.50 protocol [*pronounced as a phrase: "Z thirty-nine-dot-fifty"*]. An international standard for client gateway software that allows a person to search and download cataloging records and information from computer servers on many types of databases and library catalogs. Both the client and server must have Z39.50 software installed for downloading to take place. In many cases, however, firewall ports need to be adjusted to download from outside sources. The Library of Congress maintains a Z39.50 gateway to its catalog and those at hundreds of other institutions throughout the world at https://www.loc.gov/z3950/.

ABOUT THE EDITORS AND CONTRIBUTORS

EDITORS

Michele Zwierski, lead editor of this book, is the manager of cataloging services for the Nassau Library System on Long Island, NY. After receiving her MLS from the University of North Texas, she practiced as a cataloger specializing in nonprint materials at academic libraries in Virginia, Connecticut, and Texas before joining the Austin Public Library as a branch manager. Michele has taught cataloging courses at the University of Texas at Austin and at the Palmer School of Library and Information Science at LIU Post. In addition to her current cataloging and managerial responsibilities, she presents workshops on a variety of library service topics. Michele has been a long-standing supporter of the Cataloging of Children's Materials Committee (CCMC) and is currently chair of the Dewey Editorial Policy Committee. She has contributed to several publications, including the fifth edition of *Cataloging Correctly for Kids*. Michele also plays bass in several community orchestras on Long Island, having earned a Bachelor of Music degree from the University of Wisconsin-Madison, and a Master of Arts degree at the Yale School of Music before beginning her library career.

Joanna F. Fountain consults with librarians, especially those working with children's and bilingual collections, and is an editor, contributor, and publisher of related publications. She taught at The University of Texas at Austin (UT

Austin), and online at San José State University, Sam Houston State University, and other universities. Previously she directed technical services at the university and school-district levels, and led Proyecto LEER at the Texas Woman's University, where she earned her PhD. She organized several special libraries, was editorial director for Voluntad Publishers, a branch librarian for the Austin Public Library, and school librarian at Emerson Elementary School in Florida. She was co-editor of earlier editions of *Cataloging Correctly for Kids*, compiled *Subject Headings for School and Public Libraries*, and co-authored editions of *Unlocking the Mysteries of Cataloging: A Workbook of Examples*. Born in Mexico and the daughter of missionary publishers, she attended Howard College (Samford University) in Birmingham, AL, and earned a BA from Syracuse University and an MLS from UT Austin. A member of the CCMC for many years, she is currently a member of the Texas Library Association and ALA. She loves being semi-retired, enjoying gardening, reading, and finally spending real time with her grown daughter and calico cat.

Marilyn McCroskey retired in November 2020 from Meyer Library, Missouri State University (MSU), Springfield, where she served as professor and head of cataloging. She holds a BS in education and an MA in English from MSU and an MA in library science from the University of Missouri. She joined the MSU faculty in 1981, after five years as a school librarian for grades 7-12. She regularly taught cataloging courses at MSU until 2014, when the LIS program was discontinued. Since 1981, her own cataloging work has included children's nonbook materials for MSU's Greenwood Laboratory School and for the curriculum resource center used by the College of Education. She first joined CCMC in 2008 and has served as a member for most of the years since (except as required by CCMC's term limits). She authored a book on audiovisual cataloging, *Cataloging Nonbook Materials with AACR2 and MARC: A Guide for the School Library Media Specialist*, for the American Association of School Librarians in 1994, and a second edition in 1999, both of which were published by ALA. She has presented nonbook cataloging in-service sessions at conferences and school librarians' meetings. In addition to her supervisory work, writing, and teaching, she served on the Cataloging in Publication (CIP) Advisory Group for the Library of Congress 2000-2020. She served as an elected member of the Marionville (Missouri) R-9 Board of Education for twenty-four years, ending this work in 2016. She has been a member of ALA, ALCTS, AASL, and OLAC. She lives with her husband on a dairy farm twenty-five miles southwest of Springfield, MO. She has three children, five grandchildren, and a greatgranddaughter. She enjoys reading mystery novels.

CONTRIBUTORS

Emily Creo is head of cataloging for the Four County Library System in Vestal, NY, as well as music librarian for the Binghamton Community Orchestra. She is responsible for cataloging an eclectic variety of kits, toys, games, and educational tools for forty-two public libraries. She is the current vice president/president-elect of OLAC and chair of the CCMC. Emily received her MSLS from Clarion University of Pennsylvania, and an MM in music history and literature from Binghamton University. When not cataloging, she is an avid Anglophile, cellist, and nature enthusiast. She also enjoys spending time with her husband and two rescue dogs.

Lesley S. J. Farmer is a professor at California State University (CSU) Long Beach, where she coordinates the Teacher Librarianship program and has been named as the university's Outstanding Professor. She also manages the CSU ICT Literacy Project. She earned her MS in library science at the University of North Carolina at Chapel Hill and received her doctorate in adult education from Temple University. She chaired the IFLA's School Libraries Section and is a Fulbright Scholar. A frequent presenter and writer for the profession, she has won several honors, including ALA's Phi Beta Mu Award for library education, the International Association of School Librarianship Commendation Award, and the Anne Gellar Award from the Special Library Association's Education Division. Lesley's research interests include digital citizenship, information literacy, and data analytics.

Allison G. Kaplan is a faculty associate in the Information School at the University of Wisconsin-Madison, where she teaches courses in cataloging, reference, and children's literature. She has a doctorate in educational leadership from the University of Delaware and master's degrees in library and information science and in dance from the University of California, Los Angeles. Allison was a cataloger for over twenty years and is the author of *Catalog It! A Guide to Cataloging School Library Materials* (3rd edition, Libraries Unlimited, 2016).

Alex Kyrios is an editor of the Dewey Decimal Classification at OCLC. In this capacity, he serves as a liaison to the Subject Analysis Committee (SAC) and the CCMC, as well as the European DDC Users Group (EDUG). He previously worked as a cataloger at the University of Idaho and the Folger Shakespeare Library. He received his MLS at the School of Information and Library Science at the University of North Carolina at Chapel Hill, and his BA at the College of William & Mary. In his spare time, he contributes to Wikipedia, hosts bar trivia, and enjoys games of all sorts. He lives in Washington, DC.

Patricia Ratkovich is an assistant professor and catalog librarian in resource acquisition and discovery at the University of Alabama in Tuscaloosa, where she has served for more than two decades. She has been active in the Planning Committee, and Liaison to the Committee on Cataloging: Description and Access (CC:DA), and the CCMC. She compiled and published *Resources for Catalogers of Children's Materials* with Lynne Jacobson for the CCMC.

Caroline Saccucci is the chief of the U.S. Programs, Law, and Literature Division, Acquisitions and Bibliographic Access Directorate, Library of Congress. Prior to her current appointment, she was the program manager and section head of the Cataloging in Publication (CIP) and Dewey Section in the U.S. Programs, Law, and Literature Division, Acquisitions and Bibliographic Access Directorate, Library of Congress. She has been a member of the ALCTS Public Libraries Technical Services Interest Group, the CCMC, and the ALCTS Leadership Development Committee. She is the LC Dewey Program Liaison to the ALCTS CaMMS Subject Analysis Committee and the LC representative to the Dewey Decimal Classification Editorial Policy Committee. She is a Library's appointed member of the IFLA Standing Committee on Subject Access and Analysis. She has co-authored articles published by *Cataloging and Classification Quarterly* and *Library Resources and Technical Services.* She has a BA in history from Longwood University (Virginia) and an MLS from Simmons College. She is also active in the classical music world as an amateur violist.

Trina Soderquist is a cataloger for the Children's and Young Adults' Cataloging (CYAC) Program in the U.S. Programs, Law, and Literature Division at the Library of Congress in Washington, DC. Before joining LC, she worked as the cataloger at the Educational Resource Center, the K-12 curriculum library serving the School of Education at Boston College in Chestnut Hill, MA, where she handled curriculum materials in all formats and children's fiction and nonfiction literature. She has participated in OLAC and in the CCMC. She is a frequent user of library resources and holds library cards from several Washington-area public libraries. She lives just outside the Beltway with her husband and son.

Raegan Wiechert holds an MLS from the University of Missouri-Columbia. She is an assistant professor and cataloger at Missouri State University. She has fifteen years of cataloging experience and has previously co-authored *Crash Course in Basic Cataloging with RDA* with Heather Moulaison. For the past year, she has been leading the cataloging portion of MSU's migration from III Sierra to FOLIO library software. She is a member of the CCMC and has previously served on other ALCTS committees and task forces. In her free time, she enjoys reading and shopping. The obligatory cat is Anne.

INDEX